NEW DIRECTIONS FOR ADULT AND CONTINUING EDUCATION

Susan Imel, *Ohio State University*
EDITOR-IN-CHIEF

Contemporary Viewpoints on Teaching Adults Effectively

Jovita M. Ross-Gordon
University of South Florida

EDITOR

Number 93, Spring 2002

JOSSEY-BASS
San Francisco

CONTEMPORARY VIEWPOINTS ON TEACHING ADULTS EFFECTIVELY
Jovita M. Ross-Gordon (ed.)
New Directions for Adult and Continuing Education, no. 93
Susan Imel, Editor-in-Chief

Microfilm copies of issues and articles are available in 16mm and 35mm, as well as microfiche in 105mm, through University Microfilms Inc., 300 North Zeeb Road, Ann Arbor, Michigan 48106-1346.

ISSN 1520-3247   electronic ISSN   ISBN 0-7879-6229-5

NEW DIRECTIONS FOR ADULT AND CONTINUING EDUCATION is part of The Jossey-Bass Higher and Adult Education Series and is published quarterly by Wiley Subscription Services, Inc., a Wiley company, at Jossey-Bass, 989 Market Street, San Francisco, California 94103-1741. Periodicals postage paid at San Francisco, California, and at additional mailing offices. Postmaster: Send address changes to New Directions for Adult and Continuing Education, Jossey-Bass, 989 Market Street, San Francisco, California, 94103-1741.

SUBSCRIPTIONS cost $65.00 for individuals and $135.00 for institutions, agencies, and libraries.

EDITORIAL CORRESPONDENCE should be sent to the Editor-in-Chief, Susan Imel, ERIC/ACVE, 1900 Kenny Road, Columbus, Ohio 43210-1090. e-mail: imel.l@osu.edu.

Cover photograph by Wernher Krutein/PHOTOVAULT © 1990.

www.josseybass.com

Printed in the United States of America on acid-free recycled paper containing 100 percent recovered waste paper, of which at least 20 percent is postconsumer waste.

CONTENTS

EDITOR'S NOTES

Ask the average person the meaning of the term *adult educator,* and chances are that the person's definition will focus on the role of adult educator as a teacher—someone responsible for guiding the learning of adult learners. Those who have worked as adult educators or studied the literature of the field are likely to mention other roles and functions of the adult educator as well, such as developing and administering educational programs or educational and career counseling. Yet even for those experienced in the field and knowledgeable of its literature, the role of teacher is likely to remain front and center in describing the work of the adult educator. Hence, this issue was planned to focus on this critical adult educator role.

This issue reflects approaches and perspectives on teaching adults shared by authors who have published books related to adult teaching and learning during the past decade. One influential trend, that of highlighting the interconnections between teaching and learning, became apparent in the initial efforts to invite as chapter authors those who had theorized and published books specifically on teaching, with the idea that other books have focused more specifically on adult learning. It soon became apparent that this was to some degree an artificial separation, as demonstrated by several chapters ultimately selected for inclusion in this issue because of, rather than in spite of, their integrated treatments of teaching and learning. As terms like *learner-centered teaching* and *teaching for active learning* have become prominent in both higher and adult education practice and literature, so too has the realization that engaging in student-centered teaching requires both a keen understanding of adult learning and a willingness to simultaneously take on the role of learner.

This issue brings together the perspectives of nine experts on the teaching of adults who have published book-length works related to the subject. The chapters share a focus on understanding what constitutes effective teaching of adults rather than an emphasis on the techniques that constitute the teacher's toolkit. (Excellent sources on methods and strategies for adult training and teaching include Galbraith, 1990; Seaman and Fellenz, 1990; Davis and Davis, 1998; and Taylor, Marienau, and Fiddler, 2000.) At the same time, the implications for teaching practice will be evident in each chapter.

The first two chapters provide an introduction to the issue and set out a framework for readers to reflect on the beliefs, values, and assumptions guiding their own teaching practice. The next five chapters separately examine dimensions of the teaching-learning transaction that have received particular attention during the past decade: teaching for transformation, teaching as a dialogic process, teaching as mentoring, race as a variable in the teaching-learning transaction, and accommodating the learning needs of all. The final chapter synthesizes the themes and issues that these authors raise and integrates them into a broader context.

In Chapter One, Pratt cautions against a one-size-fits-all approach to the teaching of adults, whether it is the constructivist view of learning and teaching popular today or some other view of teaching and learning. Based on conclusions from ten years of research in five countries, documented more extensively in *Five Perspectives on Teaching in Adult and Higher Education* (Pratt and others, 1998), he delineates five distinct perspectives on teaching, each with the potential to inform good teaching: transmission, developmental (linked to the constructivist orientation), apprenticeship, nurturing, and social reform. Each represents a legitimate view of teaching that may serve as the core of good teaching when it is accompanied by reflection on the purposes guiding one's practices as a teacher.

Heimlich and Norland's discussion of teaching style in Chapter Two similarly reminds us that there is not a single approach to teaching adults. As they note, the "study of teaching style focuses on the beliefs, values, and behaviors of educators as they relate to the way the elements of the teaching learning exchange [teacher, learner, group, content, and environment] function." They maintain that congruence between the educator's philosophy and behavior in the teaching-learning exchange is the central element in understanding teaching style. (This chapter provides a condensed version of their work explored in their *Developing Teaching Style in Adult Education* [1994].)

In Chapter Three, Zachary explores the relationship between the role of mentor and the role of teacher, acknowledging that while good teaching practice informs good mentoring and vice versa, these roles are not synonymous and not all teachers either seek or serve adeptly in the role of mentor. She emphasizes the importance of relationship to mentoring and the centrality of effective facilitation skills to promoting effective learning within a mentoring relationship.

Zachary suggests that teachers should be prepared to navigate five phases of the mentoring relationship: (1) preparing oneself for the relationship, (2) preparing the relationship, (3) negotiating, (4) enabling, and (5) coming to closure. She suggests that even a relationship that does not end with successful completion of learning goals can benefit from having a good closure experience but that this requires planning for an exit strategy.

Johnson-Bailey in Chapter Four brings to an explicit level a dimension of the teaching-learning transaction that typically remains unacknowledged: race, of both learners and instructor. She challenges the notion of the adult education classroom as a neutral territory, unaffected by hierarchical power relations. She maintains that in American society race, an elusive socially defined construct, remains a potent marker used to categorize people and thus to allocate educational resource.

Johnson-Bailey identifies three major outlooks or stances with regard to race found in adult education literature—the color-blind, multicultural, and social justice perspectives—and observes that until recently, the literature of the field has been dominated by the color-blind and multicultural perspectives. Presenting the social justice perspective as an alternative, she reviews recent literature that examines the ways in which privilege and positionality affect adult education curriculum, classroom practices, and interaction between teachers and learners and among learners.

Gadbow begins Chapter Five by presenting a set of six learners, each with special learning needs that require accommodations to facilitate their success, although not all would be considered disabled in traditional terms. Drawing on these learner scenarios, she advances the notion that the responsive teacher, facilitator, or mentor can recognize all learners' possibilities as well as needs. She acknowledges that many adults who bring special needs to the learning situation also have visible or invisible disabilities that present barriers to learning. Perhaps equally important to identifying ways of accommodating the barriers, she suggests, may be assisting learners in the development of self-advocacy skills. Focusing particularly on the context of higher education, she invites readers to imagine benefits to all learners if more flexible structures, allowing a range of options for program completion, were implemented. She suggests a number of ways in which educational programs can be made responsive to special learning needs, including responsive teaching, more flexible use of technologies in distance-learning programs, and use of assistive technologies. Readers will find useful her chart identifying resources for additional information on disabilities.

Many would agree that during the 1990s, transformative learning theory replaced andragogy as the dominant theory of adult learning. Cranton offers in Chapter Six a primer on transformative learning theory and discusses the special role of critical reflection in the transformative learning process. She delineates seven facets of the process, once thought of as steps: (1) an activating event, (2) articulating assumptions, (3) critical self-reflection, (4) being open to alternative viewpoints, (5) engaging in discourse, (6) redoing assumptions, and (7) acting, thinking, and talking in a way consistent with revised assumptions. Furthermore, she proposes teaching strategies for each of the seven facets.

In Chapter Seven, Vella explores the strong connections between teaching and learning. She opens the chapter with a definition of quantum learning and follows with an outline of the companion teaching approach, referred to as the dialogue approach (Vella, 1996). She acknowledges the paradox of using a highly structured teaching approach designed to invite spontaneity. Lest such an approach be interpreted as the latest method of training the trainers, readers are encouraged to read Vella's account of the conceptual roots of quantum learning with a legacy of diverse progenitors.

Finally, Chapter Eight identifies cross-cutting themes from the previous chapters.

Collectively, the chapters in this issue should stimulate readers to reflect on many aspects of the teaching-learning situation and the social context within which adult education programs are situated, along with their personal histories and assumptions, values, and beliefs. Readers also will find strategies for aligning teaching practices with some of the core assumptions about adult teaching and learning prominent today.

References

Davis, J. R., and Davis, A. B. *Effective Training Strategies: A Comprehensive Guide to Maximizing Learning in Organizations.* San Francisco: Jossey-Bass, 1998.

Galbraith, M. *Adult Learning Methods: A Guide for Effective Instruction.* Malabar, Fla.: Krieger, 1990.

Heimlich, J. E., and Norland, E. *Developing Teaching Style in Adult Education.* San Francisco: Jossey-Bass, 1994.

Pratt, D. D., and others. *Five Perspectives on Teaching in Adult and Higher Education.* Malabar, Fla.: Krieger, 1998.

Seaman, D. F., and Fellenz, R. A. *Effective Strategies for Teaching Adults.* Columbus, Ohio: Merrill, 1990.

Taylor, K., Marineau, C., and Fiddler, M. *Developing Adult Learners: Strategies for Teachers and Trainers.* San Francisco: Jossey-Bass, 2000.

Vella, J. *Training Through Dialogue.* San Francisco: Jossey-Bass, 1996.

Jovita M. Ross-Gordon
Editor

JOVITA M. ROSS-GORDON is an associate professor in the College of Education at Southwest Texas State University, San Marcos.

1

This chapter provides a counterargument to the trend toward a new educational orthodoxy that says all teacher development should follow a constructivist path to good teaching.

Good Teaching: One Size Fits All?

Daniel D. Pratt

Across North America and, increasingly, the rest of the world, there is a move within education to adopt a constructivist view of learning and teaching. In part, the argument for this move is a reaction against teacher-centered instruction that has dominated much of education, particularly adult and higher education, for the past forty years or more. Although I do not argue with the basic tenets of constructivism, I do resist the rush to adopt a single dominant view of learning or teaching. Unless we are cautious, I fear we are about to replace one orthodoxy with yet another and promote a one-size-fits-all notion of good teaching.

My caution is derived from ten years of research in five different countries, studying hundreds of teachers of adults. Across a wide range of disciplines, contexts, and cultures, my colleagues and I found a plurality of good teaching, not all of which rests on constructivist principles of learning. Our findings are not unique. They correspond to those of many other researchers around the world, as far back as Fox (1983) and as recently as Grubb and others (1999). In reviewing most of that research, Kember (1997) found a surprisingly high level of correspondence across countries and researchers. No single view of learning or teaching dominated what might be called "good teaching."[1] In our research, we documented five perspectives on teaching, each with the potential to be good teaching: transmission, developmental, apprenticeship, nurturing, and social reform (Pratt and others, 1998).

I thank Robert Rubeck and John Collins for their comments about and contributions to this chapter.

Five Perspectives on Teaching

A perspective on teaching is an interrelated set of beliefs and intentions that gives direction and justification to our actions. It is a lens through which we view teaching and learning. We may not be aware of our perspective because it is something we look through, rather than look at, when teaching. Each of the perspectives in this chapter is a unique blend of beliefs, intentions, and actions. Yet there is overlap among them. Similar actions, intentions, and even beliefs can be found in more than one perspective. Teachers holding different perspectives may, for example, have similar beliefs about the importance of critical reflection in work and educational contexts. To this end, all may espouse the use of higher-level questions as a means of promoting critical thinking. However, the way questions are asked and the way in which teachers listen and respond when people consider those questions may vary considerably across perspectives. These variations are also directly related to our beliefs about learning, knowledge, and the appropriate role of an instructor.

It is common for people to confuse perspectives on teaching with methods of teaching. Some say they use all five perspectives at one time or another, depending on circumstances. On the surface, this seems reasonable. However, a deeper look reveals that perspectives are far more than methods. In part, this confusion derives from the fact that the same teaching actions are common across perspectives: lecturing, discussion, questioning, and a host of other methods are common activities within all five perspectives. It is how they are used, and toward what ends, that differentiates perspectives.

Based on data from over two thousand teachers who have taken the Teaching Perspectives Inventory (Pratt and Collins, 2000), we know that over 90 percent of teachers hold only one or two perspectives as their dominant view of teaching and only marginally identify with one or two others. It could not be otherwise, given that perspectives vary in their views of knowledge, learning, and teaching.

What follows is a snapshot of each perspective, including a metaphor for the adult learner and a set of key beliefs, primary responsibilities, typical strategies, and common difficulties. Each snapshot is a composite of many representative people. Therefore, it would be unlikely that any one individual would have all the characteristics listed for any one perspective. As you read them, try to locate yourself not by looking for a perfect fit but for the best fit. Which of the perspectives seems to capture your own orientation toward teaching and learning? I expect you will find parts of each perspective that fit but that the overall profile of one or two snapshots will feel more comfortable than others.[2]

A Transmission Perspective. The transmission perspective is the most common orientation to teaching in secondary and higher education, though not in elementary and adult education. From the transmission perspective, effective teaching starts with a substantial commitment to the content or subject matter, so it is essential for transmission-oriented teachers to have mastery over their content.

Many who teach from this perspective hold certain assumptions and views of adults as learners. Some tend to think of the adult learner as a "container" to be filled with something (knowledge). This knowledge exists outside the learner, usually within the text or in the teacher. Teachers are to efficiently and effectively pass along (teach) a common body of knowledge and way of thinking similar to what is in the text or the teacher.

Such a process of learning is additive, meaning that teachers should take care not to overload their learners with too much information. To increase the amount that is learned, teachers should focus their presentations on the internal structure of the content. This structure can then be used as an effective means of storing and retrieving the material. With proper delivery by the teacher and proper receptivity by the learner, knowledge can be transferred from the teacher to the learner.

From the transmission perspective, learners are expected to learn the content in its authorized or legitimate forms, and teachers are expected to take learners systematically through a set of tasks that lead to mastery of the content. To do this, teachers, beginning with the fundamentals, must provide clear objectives and well-organized lectures, adjust the pace of lecturing, make efficient use of class time, clarify misunderstandings, answer questions, correct errors, provide reviews, summarize what has been presented, direct students to appropriate resources, set high standards for achievement, and develop objective means of assessing learning. How do effective transmission teachers accomplish this? What strategies do they use?

First, transmission teachers spend a lot of time in preparation, ensuring their mastery over the content to be presented. They specify what students should learn (objectives) and take care to see that resources and assignments are in line with those objectives. Their goal is to pass on to learners a specific body of knowledge or skill as efficiently and effectively as possible. In order to accommodate individual differences, they vary the pace of instruction, sometimes speeding up and other times slowing down or repeating what was said. Feedback to learners is directed at errors and pointing out where learners can improve their performance. Assessment of learning is usually a matter of locating learners within a hierarchy of knowledge or skill to be learned.

As with all other perspectives, teachers holding transmission as their dominant perspective have some difficulties. For example, they often find it difficult to work with people who do not understand the logic of their content. This causes difficulty anticipating where and why learners are likely to struggle with the content. In addition, many whom we studied had difficulty thinking of examples or problems from the world outside the classroom as a means of making their content come to life. And when challenged by learners, they often returned to the content as a means of dealing with those challenges. Finally, it was not unusual in our observations to see transmission teachers spend too much time talking. In fact, it seemed that many used learner responses or questions as an opportunity to talk some more. These teachers were primarily focused on the content rather than the learners.

Much of this description sounds negative, and, indeed, most of us can think of teachers who fit well in this perspective and were less than stellar. Transmission orientations to teaching provide some of the most common negative examples of teaching. Nevertheless, many of us also have positive memories of teachers who were passionate about the content, animated in its delivery, and determined that we go away with respect and enthusiasm for their subject. Such an individual may have inspired us to take up a particular vocation or field of study. Their deep respect and enthusiasm for the subject was infectious. It is the memory of those teachers that must be preserved if we are to see transmission as a legitimate perspective on teaching.

A Developmental Perspective. The constructivist orientation to learning is the foundation for this perspective on teaching. From the developmental perspective, the primary goal of education or training is to develop increasingly complex and sophisticated ways of reasoning and problem solving within a content area or field of practice.

A typical metaphor for understanding the adult learner is the computer. From this perspective, teachers need to know how their learners are "programmed," that is, how they think and what they believe in relation to the content or work. With that information, teachers try to build bridges from the learners' way of thinking to better, more complex, and more sophisticated ways of thinking and reasoning. The assumption behind this strategy is that learning brings about one of two kinds of change inside the brain. First, when a new experience fits with what someone already knows, it builds a stronger and more elaborate pathway to that knowledge. Second, if a new experience or new content does not fit the learner's current way of knowing, she or he must either change the old way of knowing or reject the new knowledge or experience. The goal is to change the way learners think rather than increase their store of knowledge.

Behind this view lies a constructivist tenet that learners use what they already know to filter and interpret new information. In effect, this means that learners construct their understanding rather than reproduce the teacher's understanding. Making sense of the world by relating it to what one already knows has implications for teaching. Foremost, it means that teachers must genuinely value learners' prior knowledge and understand how they think about the content before presenting new material. Once this is accomplished, developmental teachers employ two common strategies: the judicious use of effective questioning that challenges learners to move from relatively simple to more complex forms of thinking and the use of meaningful examples. Questions, problems, cases, and examples form the bridge that teachers use to transport learners from previous ways of thinking and reasoning to new, more complex, and sophisticated forms of reasoning and problem solving. Approaching instruction in this way has implications for the use of teachers' knowledge. Developmental teachers adapt their knowledge to learners' ways of understanding.

It is not easy to teach from this perspective, as teachers trying to change from a transmission to developmental orientation will attest. For example, asking good questions, the kind that require time to think and reason before answering, is not easy. And after asking the question, waiting while learners think and voice their thoughts takes patience. It is difficult to refrain from telling learners rather than letting them figure it out for themselves, especially when teachers know the answer. However, the most common difficulty that teachers have when trying to teach from this perspective is in developing practice and assessment tasks that are consistent with complex reasoning. They tend to focus on recall, recognition, and correct answers rather than on reflection, analysis, and reasoning.

Increasingly, teachers at all levels of education are espousing this perspective on teaching. It has become the new orthodoxy and is also the basis for much of the progressive movement of problem- and case-based learning in the professions. The central commitment to the learner's level of knowledge and skill as a starting point is laudable and effective. However, the progression from espousing to enacting a developmental perspective involves much more than a repertoire of techniques for engaging learners in problems and discussion. It also means that teachers must use their knowledge and expertise in ways that do not undermine the goal of helping learners construct their own forms of understanding. Indeed, from this perspective, sometimes less (telling) means more (learning).

An Apprenticeship Perspective. The apprenticeship view of teaching may be familiar to many, especially those who have gone through an apprenticeship or internship. As we learn more about why so little classroom learning transfers to work sites, this view becomes increasingly relevant. From an apprenticeship perspective, learning is facilitated when people work on authentic tasks in real settings of application or practice. Although this is difficult to do in a classroom, some teachers have accomplished this in classrooms (Collins, Brown, and Holum, 1991).

Whether in classrooms or at work sites, the instructor is responsible for revealing the inner workings of skilled performance. This is part of the transition apprenticeship teachers must make when moving from doing the work to teaching about doing it. Performing is different from teaching about performing. Teachers must find ways to translate the habituated movement and artistry of performance into language and demonstrations that are accessible and meaningful to learners.

From an apprenticeship perspective, learning is more than the building of cognitive structures or the development of skilled competence. It is, as well, the transformation of the learners' identity that occurs as they adopt the language, values, and practices of a specific social group. In the language of collaborative learning and social constructivism, this is the same process teachers take students through when reenculturating them into a new community of practice way of thinking (Bruffee, 1999). A useful metaphor for thinking about the learner, then, is as an outsider using education and training as a means of entry to practice. However, from this perspective, learners are also using education or training as a means of learning a new discourse of action and identity.

Learning therefore is a matter of developing competence and identity in relation to other members of a community of practice. Learners' progress is marked by their skilled performance and their movement from the periphery (as novice or beginner) to the center (as experienced members) of the social life and practices of a community. As new members come into a community, the community itself undergoes changes in defining and enacting appropriate roles, responsibilities, and relationships. Thus, three central tenets of this view are that learning is a process of enculturation, knowledge is socially constructed through participation in a social group, and the product of learning is of two kinds: competence and social identity in relation to the community of practice.

The instructor's responsibility is to see that learners work on tasks that are meaningful and relevant to the community of practice. One of the principal strategies by which they do this is scaffolding: breaking the performance or work into tasks and sequences that progress from simple and marginal to complex and central to the work of the community. Ideally, all of the scaffolding of learning should be integral to the work and legitimate in the eyes of other workers.

At the same time, instructors have another responsibility: reading their learners' point of entry and capability in relation to the work, which Vygotsky (1978) called finding their "zone of proximal development." In more conventional terms, it means knowing the difference between what learners can do on their own and what they can do with guided assistance from the instructor. This is their zone of development, but it is also the teacher's zone of instruction. As learners make progress, the zone moves with the learners, defining new boundaries of autonomous and guided competence.

As learners mature and become more competent, the instructor's role changes. Tasks are still chosen based on the learner's zone of development, but over time, instructors offer less direction and give more responsibility as learners move from dependent to independent workers. Making the change from performing while learners watch to scaffolding the work according to learners' zone of development is a difficult transition for teachers. Finding the right balance between zones of development and scaffolding of work takes time and patience.

Because of this, the most common difficulty facing teachers is finding relevant and authentic tasks for classroom instruction. This is usually accomplished with cases or problems drawn from real contexts and situations of practice. However, it is not easy to develop authentic tasks at varying levels of learner competence. Another troubling aspect, even in work sites, is that of matching learners' capabilities with tasks that represent legitimate work. This is one of the keys to good teaching, yet it is encumbered by competing demands for quality work and quality teaching. Issues of safety and quality routinely intrude on teaching. Finally, many instructors find it difficult to put their knowledge or skill into words. They often say, "I know what to do, but it's difficult telling others how I do it." This difficulty is most common in skill-based occupations but is also evident in jobs that require complex reasoning. The longer we have been doing complex tasks, the more routine they become. The more routine they are, the less we need to articulate what we do. We just do it. And that is precisely what learners need to do too.

A Nurturing Perspective. The nurturing perspective assumes that long-term, diligent, persistent efforts to achieve come from the heart, not the head. People become motivated and productive learners when they are working on issues or problems without fear of failure. Learners are therefore nurtured by the knowledge that their achievement is a product of their own effort and ability, rather than the benevolence of a teacher, and that their efforts to learn will be supported by their teacher and peers. The more there is pressure to achieve and the more difficult the material is to be learned, the more important is such support for learning.

Because many adults come to further education and training with wounds from previous schooling, the working metaphor of the learner here is the vulnerable self. This metaphor is based on the belief that when a learner's self-concept is under threat or diminished in any way, learning will be blocked, diverted, or halted altogether. Desired learning outcomes therefore include more self-sufficient and confident learners, believing in the power of their own actions to achieve the learning they seek. And the primary responsibility of nurturing teachers is to find a balance between caring and challenging. To do this, they promote a climate of caring and trust, helping people set reasonable but challenging goals, and supporting effort and achievement. Above all else, they are cautious not to sacrifice self-efficacy in favor of academic achievement. Success must be clearly and consistently due to learners' ability and effort, not the benevolence of the teacher, if learners are to become less vulnerable and more competent.

Typical nurturing strategies include such simple things as getting to know people, consistently listening and responding to emotional as well as intellectual needs, and working with permeable role boundaries—for example, teaching versus counseling. Nurturing teachers provide a great deal of encouragement and support, along with clear expectations and reasonable goals for each learner. And their assessment of learning often considers individual growth or progress, as well as absolute achievement.

People often misunderstand this point and assume that nurturing teachers exempt their learners from external standards or examinations. On the contrary, external forms of accountability are presented as reasonable and achievable, especially if they are part of a program or certification requirement. Learners are encouraged to see that it is doing them no favor to be excused from being evaluated. Instead, they are helped to prepare, usually in small approximations that are both challenging and achievable, and then are encouraged to take their tests.

Nurturing forms of teaching are fraught with difficulties. First, evaluation is difficult, especially when institutional expectations run counter to an instructor's perception of what is needed to promote success with learners. Second, for many teachers, keeping the boundaries between teaching and counseling permeable is a problem. They often give too much of themselves and in the end suffer for it.

In addition, many find themselves defending the nurturing perspective against their colleagues' criticisms. Its very name has feminine connotations, and some view it as suggesting lower standards. Yet for those who are most exemplary of this perspective, there is no lowering of standards. Quite the contrary; they make reasonable demands and set high expectations for their learners. For them, caring does not negate having high expectations.

The balance between caring and challenging is difficult to achieve and sustain, especially with a diverse group of learners. Some nurturing teachers never do find it and succumb to the most common ailment of this perspective: wanting (too much) to be liked by their students. However, for the good teachers, the overriding goal is to help people feel good about their achievements and believe in themselves as learners. It is the reversal of these means and ends that most defines this perspective. For nurturing teachers, achievement is only the means by which people can improve their self-confidence and self-esteem as learners. Because of this, these teachers are never willing to sacrifice self-esteem on the altar of achievement.

A Social Reform Perspective. The social reform perspective is the most difficult one to describe because it has no single, uniform characteristics or set of strategies. In our research, we found social reform teachers in community development, Native education, AIDS awareness, Mothers Against Drunk Driving, the civil rights movement, environmental education, women's health, labor union education, religious education, and even within such established occupations and professions as automotive repair and medical education. In every instance, the teacher we met was either a leader or a rebel.

At first glance, effective social reform teachers have much in common with other effective teachers. They are clear and organized in their delivery of content, bring learners into diverse communities of practice, ask probing questions and use powerful metaphors that help learners bridge between prior knowledge and new concepts, and work hard to respect and promote the dignity and self-efficacy of their learners.

These skills and attributes are not, however, the defining qualities of social reform teachers. They are instead the means by which these teachers work toward a set of ideals. It is a particularly strong set of ideals that distinguishes their orientation and is ultimately the measure of their teaching. When social reform teachers are effective, those ideals are explicitly and profoundly related to the lives of their learners. For the teaching to be judged effective, learners must come to believe that the guiding ideals are as important to them as they are to the teacher. Social reform teachers seek not just to interpret the world, but to change it in ways that correspond to their ideals.

Social reform teachers make three assumptions: that their ideals are necessary for a better society, that their ideals are appropriate for all, and that the ultimate goal of teaching is to bring about social change, not simply individual learning. The collective, rather than the individual, is the object of change. Social reform teachers are unequivocal and clear about what changes are desired and necessary. They see themselves as instruments of social change and are known among their colleagues and students as advocates for the changes they wish to bring about in society.

Social reform teachers encourage students to consider the ways in which they, as learners of the discipline they are studying, are positioned and constructed in particular discourses of practice. Common practices within a discipline or field of study are examined for their implicit values and the ways in which those practices reproduce and maintain untenable conditions. Texts and practices are interrogated for what is said and what is not said, what is included and what is excluded, and who is represented and who is not represented in the dominant discourses of practice. Classroom discussion is centered not on knowledge itself or how knowledge has been created, but by whom and for what purposes. Subject matter content therefore is not just taught; it is interrogated for its complicity in the malaise of society. However, the critical deconstruction of text and common practices, though central to this perspective on teaching, is not an end in itself. The purpose of encouraging students to take a critical stance is to give them power to take social action to improve their own lives.

Teachers who embody the social reform perspective are few and far between. But those who do are very likely to have a lasting impression on their learners. We may have had a teacher who caused us to question things we took for granted, about ourselves or about society at large. It may have been the first critical theory course we took, or a feminist educator we knew, or a spiritual leader who caused us to rethink our deepest assumptions and convictions. In any case, like the other perspectives, this orientation to teaching can be wonderful or dreadful, depending on the quality of teaching and our readiness to embrace its underlying values.

Applying Awareness of the Perspectives to Improving Teaching

Perspectives are neither good nor bad. They are simply philosophical orientations to knowledge, learning, and the role and responsibility of being a teacher. Therefore, it is important to remember that each of these perspectives represents a legitimate view of teaching when enacted appropriately. Conversely, each holds the potential for poor teaching. However, if teachers are to improve, they must reflect on what they do, why they do it, and on what grounds those actions and intentions are justified. Besides resisting a one-size-fits-all approach to development and evaluation, how can these perspectives help in that process?

For several years, educators of adults have been admonished to reflect critically on the underlying assumptions and values that give direction and justification to their work. This is not an easy task. What is it that we are to reflect on? How are our underlying values and assumptions to be identified? In other words, the objects of critical reflection are not self-evident. Indeed, it is something of a twist to look not only at our teaching but at the very lenses through which we view our teaching.

In our work with educators, we use these perspectives as a means of helping people identify, articulate, and, if necessary, justify their approach to teaching. In this process, it also helps them thoughtfully revisit assumptions and beliefs they hold regarding learning, knowledge, and teaching. I believe this is what faculty development should be rather than the mastery of technique. Throughout the process, preconceived notions of "good teaching" are challenged as educators are asked to consider what teaching means to them.

Notes

1. I realize the phrase *good teaching* is loaded with subjectivity and may be unacceptable to some. However, the word *good* is probably the most frequently used scale point to indicate an acceptable or expected level of performance in learner and peer evaluations of teaching. In most instances, the qualifier *good* corresponds to a quality of teaching that is more than adequate though not necessarily outstanding or excellent. In my experience, it is also the threshold that all teachers, regardless of their context or disciplinary home, are expected to achieve.

2. A much more detailed description of all five perspectives is provided in Pratt and others (1998). The Teaching Perspectives Inventory can be accessed at www.teaching perspectives.com.

References

Bruffee, K. A. *Collaborative Learning: Higher Education, Interdependence, and the Authority of Knowledge.* (2nd ed.) Baltimore, Md.: Johns Hopkins University Press, 1999.

Collins, A., Brown, J. S., and Holum, A. "Cognitive Apprenticeship: Making Thinking Visible." *American Educator*, Winter 1991, pp. 6–46.

Fox, D. "Personal Theories of Teaching." *Studies in Higher Education*, 1983, 8, 151–163.

Grubb, W. N., and others. *Honored But Invisible: An Inside Look at Teaching in Community Colleges.* New York: Routledge, 1999.

Kember, D. "A Reconceptualisation of the Research into University Academics' Conceptions of Teaching." *Learning and Instruction,* 1997, 7, 255–275.

Pratt, D. D. "Conceptions of Teaching." *Adult Education Quarterly,* 1992, 42, 203–220.

Pratt, D. D., and Collins, J. B. "The Teaching Perspectives Inventory." In *Proceedings of the Forty-First Adult Education Research Conference.* Vancouver, B.C., 2000. (ED 452 417)

Pratt, D. D., and others. *Five Perspectives on Teaching in Adult and Higher Education.* Malabar, Fla.: Krieger, 1998.

Vygotsky, L. S. *Mind in Society: The Development of Higher Psychological Processes.* Cambridge, Mass.: Harvard University Press, 1978.

DANIEL D. PRATT is professor of adult and higher education in the Department of Educational Studies at the University of British Columbia, Vancouver, Canada.

2

Understanding one's teaching style can serve as a foundation for the improvement of instruction and serves not only learners but also the educator.

Teaching Style: Where Are We Now?

Joe E. Heimlich, Emmalou Norland

Teaching style is a phrase sometimes used to describe different things. Although some authors use it as if it is synonymous with *teaching method* or *technique,* most researchers who have defined *teaching style* refer to style as a predilection toward teaching behavior and the congruence between an educator's teaching behaviors and teaching beliefs (Heimlich and Norland, 1994), a pervasive quality in the educational activities of an educator that persists even when content changes (Fisher and Fisher, 1979), the distinct qualities a teacher displays that are persistent (Conti, 1998), or the characteristic ways each individual collects, organizes, and transforms information into useful knowledge (Cross, 1979). Consistent in the definitions offered by Solomon and Miller (1961), Gauld (1982), Dunn and Dunn (1979), Draves (1997), Zinn (1998), and others is the same quality of constancy of behaviors of the educator regardless of the setting or the content. Style is not method but something larger that relates to the entire teaching-learning exchange.

In any educational event, several elements are constant: there is an educator who conveys or facilitates the content to each learner and the group of learners within a situation that is both physical and the affective reaction to the physical environment. These five elements—teacher, learner, group, content, and environment—comprise a model of the teaching-learning exchange. All elements are present in every teaching-learning event or exchange, but the relationships and the importance of each component vary. Part of the variance depends on the situation and, more important, the way in which the educator operationalizes personal beliefs regarding the relationship and importance of each component. The study of teaching style focuses on the beliefs, values, and behaviors of educators as they relate to the way the elements of the exchange function.

The purpose of teaching is to enhance learning, and everything an educator does to enhance learning is of value. Most educators understand that all learners have different preferences and styles of learning and believe that it is important to teach using techniques and strategies that will satisfy the variety of learning styles in the learning event (Seaman and Fellenz, 1990). Fewer educators, however, have reflected on their own beliefs regarding the interaction around the educational event between the teacher and the learner that we call the teaching-learning exchange. Although it is important for educators to know their own beliefs and values regarding learning and teaching, it is more important for them to understand the match between their values and beliefs, or their philosophy, with their behavior in the exchange. This match, or congruence, is the central element of understanding teaching style (Brookfield, 1990). The impact on learning through congruence in the teaching-learning exchange suggests that understanding style can enhance the likelihood that the exchange will be successful in both the learners' and the educators' minds.

Individually, some of these elements are widely studied. A vast amount of literature exists on learning styles relating to the individual learner in the exchange. The field of communications provides a solid base for understanding the theory and application of groups and interactions to the teaching-learning exchange. The construct of content, and even the transfer of content to a learner, is widely considered in many fields. There is less research on, but still a substantial amount of guidance for, understanding the control and impact of the physical environment on the learner and on learning. The study of the teacher for the purpose of understanding the role of the educator in the exchange is far more constrained and historically has tended to be limited to the role of the teacher relative to the conveyance of content to the learner as in student-centered versus teacher-centered instruction (see, for example, Axelrod, 1970; Lenz, 1982; Nuthall and Snook, 1973) or in role behavior (such as Robinson, 1979). The study of teaching style seeks to fill this gap in the literature and provide a means by which adult educators can better work within the teaching-learning exchange to enhance the learning opportunities by looking for the constant, overall traits and qualities of the educator (Conti, 1989).

There is guidance about reflective practice (see, for example, Brookfield, 1990) and excellent guidance about teaching philosophies (see, for example, Zinn, 1994, 1998; Conti, 1998). But style is not the same as reflective practice or philosophy of teaching. Reflection is an important activity when an educator examines his or her style, but teaching style differs from reflective practice in that it is not just about behaviors, and style is different from philosophy in that it is not just about beliefs. Style is about congruence. To achieve congruence, educators must consider their values about teaching and learning and examine their beliefs regarding each of the elements of the teaching-learning exchange. They must then compare this set of beliefs with their practice and work for congruence in one of several ways.

Why Should We Study Teaching Style?

There are many things about an educator we can measure—for example, training, experience, content knowledge, attitudes, beliefs, and behaviors. The question must be, What about a teacher *is not* related to his or her teaching style? We can, and do, study many pieces about the teacher; studying teaching style puts the pieces together for the benefit of the individual educator and ultimately the benefit of each learner that educator touches.

One major concern is that in much of the study of adult educators, we are not treating the educator as a lifelong learner. From Knowles's (1980) assumptions to Brookfield's (1986) goals for adult educators, the field of adult education has defined certain aspects of what is necessary to understand learners. The understanding of the lifelong learner should and must extend to ourselves as the teachers of adults. One of the things all adult educators can and should continue to study is themselves—and the application of the resultant understanding to their teaching. The study of style is important because adult educators want to ensure the best learning experience for adult learners, knowing that the better the experience is, the more likely it is that learning will occur. The study of style is also important to ensure the best experience for those who teach adults.

The Study of Style

The study of style starts with what each educator holds: beliefs, values, attitudes, working philosophy, skills, and personality. The core of the individual is what makes that individual a unique, potentially powerful educator of adults. Congruence in teaching demands that the personal exploration of "who I am and what I believe" be unending. As Eble (1980) suggests, the acquisition of teaching style "is a whole and lifetime process, and . . . though style may manifest itself in skills and techniques, the development of style involves much more than these" (p. 1).

Many dimensions could be used to determine an educator's preferences and predilections in teaching. Two used to measure the beliefs about teaching are those of inclusion, which can be considered as level of control of the exchange held by the educator, and sensitivity or orientation to the five elements in a continuum of the nonhuman to the most human of considerations (Heimlich and Norland, 1994). Zinn's (1983, 1994) Philosophy of Adult Education Inventory provides a measure of the educator's philosophy regarding decisions and actions the educator holds regarding determination of the purpose and outcomes of the learning activity. Conti's (1985)

Principles of Adult Learning Scale (PALS) compares the frequency of an educator's practice with the principles described in the adult education literature. Seevers (1991) found that sensitivity and inclusion, followed by number of adult education courses taken and attitude toward being an adult educator, were the best predictors of teaching style as measured by PALS.

The exploration of teaching style ultimately involves matching the educator's behavior with his or her philosophy. Teaching style is not an excuse for bad teaching, inappropriate classroom behaviors, or the use of poorly conducted teaching methods. An underlying premise of teaching style is the understanding that although there are no "bad" styles, there are poor practices by educators. The purpose of studying style is for individual educators to understand better what they believe and how those beliefs can be congruent with their teaching behaviors in order to improve the opportunity for learning by students or participants in programs. Teaching style gives educators a starting point for exploring their own teaching.

Because style is not synonymous with method, it is important to look briefly at the study of methods. Often, educators are implored to match their methods to the content and the learner (Draves, 1997; Lovell, 1987). Good teaching always involves using a variety of methods to appeal to multiple learning orientations and senses, but all teaching methods are adaptable to every teaching style; style does not necessarily change, nor should it. How educators select their teaching strategies and implement techniques is a function of their beliefs and values regarding the methods and can be modified to fit within the unique belief system of the educator. In their purest sense, methods are not allied with the beliefs of the teacher but are a framework of processes. The manner in which any method, whether lecture or game, discovery-based learning or discussion, is used within a learning event is the choice of the educator and should be a reflection of his or her philosophy.

Options for Congruence

If the purpose of teaching style is to aid the educator in achieving congruence, then it is necessary to understand how congruence can be achieved. There are three ways in which educators who are exploring their beliefs and their behaviors can move to congruence: (1) a change of teaching behaviors, (2) a change of beliefs, or (3) a change in both or neither. The process for change in any direction starts when the educator scrutinizes his or her values and beliefs around the teaching-learning exchange and engages in deep, honest reflection on teaching choices and behaviors.

Changing Behaviors. The process by which an educator can change behaviors starts with a consideration of the variety of ways in which alterations in the teaching-learning exchange could be undertaken. The dimension of inclusion, and the belief of degree of control with which an educator manages the teaching-learning exchange, is one of the places in which an educator can most quickly identify behaviors that may not match his or her beliefs. Many educators profess a belief that learners should control the content, yet they teach using predetermined objectives and an outline of content, and they think that allowing learners to ask questions during or at the end of the teaching event equates with giving learners control in the exchange. Some educators believe that learning should be interactive and individual but in practice need to have a quiet, attentive group attending to their information and make little allowance for side discussions. Another area of behavioral change can be that of technologies used in the instructional episode. Examining the technologies used, and the beliefs that support or oppose that use, is often an area in which congruence can be enhanced.

The most obvious area for exploration is that of methods used in the exchange. In a study of nonformal adult educators, Heimlich and Meyers (1999) found that a large majority of the educators held beliefs that learners should control the exchange and be involved in the learning process. Yet over 70 percent of instruction time was spent in presentation methods (lectures and lectures with visuals). These educators held beliefs that suggested a high degree of inclusion of the learner in the learning event and low control by the educator over the learners, but the high control and low learner orientation of the predetermined lecture, even with questions and answers or visual aids, suggests dissonance between beliefs and behaviors. In practice, the need to "excuse" or "apologize" for teaching in a certain way is often an indicator of dissonance between beliefs and behaviors. Understanding the purposes of different methods and then exploring ways in which the method can better be used to match the beliefs would strengthen the teaching-learning event. There is no single correct method for any teaching style, but there are better ways in which individual educators can use various methods and the subsequent techniques and strategies.

It is impossible to view beliefs and behavior as fully separate, and it is well understood that there is interaction among affect, behavior, and cognition (Eagly and Chaiken, 1993). Yet it is possible to examine the relationships and make sense out of the relationships between behavior and beliefs and values. Most people will, with certain groups of friends or acquaintances, do things that they would not do in other situations; many routinely act one way in their professional lives and are dramatically different in their home lives. Many psychologists (and self-help books) describe the need to move to congruence in all aspects of one's life. Teaching is no different.

Changing Beliefs. The process of changing beliefs is often a more difficult, but perhaps more fundamental and long-lasting, change. Many adult educators have been instructed in a system of beliefs about teaching and learning that they may interpret as suggesting a prescribed series of beliefs. Formal education, too, has laundry lists of suggested beliefs that educators should hold: student centered is better than teacher or content centered; teach to the various learning styles of the students; engage the students in defining learning outcomes or qualities of success; and so on. Although the ideas are valid, the interpretation that there is one way to do or be that prescribed belief often constrains educators from operationalizing the concept in a manner congruent with their own beliefs.

As an illustration, any two educators can be learner centered in dramatically different ways: an educator can be high control, low sensitivity and still be oriented to the needs of the learner and be correct in the manner in which he or she is learner centered. Another educator can involve the learners in defining their learning needs, organizing their learning activities, and guiding the learning process and be no more or less student centered than the other educator. The teacher's orientation toward content also varies widely. Budak (1993) found, for example, that a teacher's philosophy was not significantly related to training, attitude toward teaching, nature of content, or physical environment but was related to experience and the status of content held by the teacher. Understanding one's personal belief system and knowing how all behaviors relate to those beliefs is an important component of exploring style.

Rokeach (1968) described beliefs as an onion skin in which the closer to the core the beliefs are held, the less likely they are to change. At the core, he suggests, there are only a few central values on which all behaviors are based and that tend to be culturally bound. The beliefs that lie further from the core are those (derived and peripheral) likely to vary depending on the situation; these beliefs are formed from experiences, family, instruction, situations, and outside influences. Sometimes these more external beliefs are professed beliefs and are assumed by an individual as the things they should believe, which Bem (1967) summarizes in his self-perception theory stating that if people perceive themselves to have certain behaviors, they will report consistent attitudes to match that perception. For adult educators, these may be the stated beliefs that echo the ideals of the profession but do not necessarily match the more deeply held beliefs of the educator. Such external beliefs are those most easily changed when the individual challenges the behaviors. Changing beliefs requires that an individual determine which values he or she holds are close to core and then look for the beliefs he or she holds about teaching and learning that first support those beliefs, and then those that contradict.

Contradictory or competing beliefs exist in all people. Yet these contradictory beliefs somehow become integrated into an individual's understanding of self. It is possible to examine the whole of a person's belief system by exploring his or her life philosophy. Zinn (1998) explains philosophy as "individual beliefs [that] generally fit into groups or categories with other similar beliefs, forming belief systems which, as a whole, comprise a life philosophy" (p. 38). The trap for many educators is to explore their beliefs around teaching and learning without placing those beliefs in the context of their larger belief systems—their lives. To suggest that educators are able to separate themselves completely from their life outside the teaching event is to deny the very human nature of teaching. The educator is a human who, by connecting with other humans, is facilitating acquisition of insights, knowledge, awareness, affect, or skills. The more fully the educator is able to integrate his or her whole self into the teaching-learning exchange, the more the focus of the exchange can be on the learning and the learning process rather than the teacher and the methods or models for teaching (Tight, 2000).

Changing Both Beliefs and Behaviors or Neither. The third option is either the most challenging or, conversely, the easy way out. If through reflection and consideration, an educator finds that her professed belief system does not match what she truly believes on a deeper level, and that her behaviors do not match what she thinks she truly believes, she can choose to change both or change neither.

Changing both suggests that an educator has found no clarity in either her current philosophy or behavior. This is not to say that an individual seeking to change both philosophy and behavior is not a good teacher, but that this person has discovered that her beliefs may be inconsistent or inherently contradictory and that what she does in a teaching event may not always feel genuine. Seeking change of both beliefs and behavior requires intense critical reflection and a willingness to grow in ways that may be somewhat difficult, at least for a while.

There are, of course, those who may find beliefs or behaviors inconsistent or forced but choose to change neither. In some cases, the fear of change or the fear of trying something new can create a barrier to an individual's willingness to change. In other situations, an educator may truly believe there is no reason to change. Challenging one's beliefs or behaviors is what we call growth as educators. Not all educators are prepared for, or willing to work on, growth at all times during their careers. Sometimes, because the teaching seems to go well, these educators may not know that they could be better teachers, or they may understand that growth requires work and choose not to explore growth at that time. In other situations, educators may understand that there is potential for growth, but they do not have the tools, resources, or access to tools and resources to know how to effect change. And there are those educators who rarely think of themselves as teachers beyond being a vessel for the content they are to convey to learners. In any of these situations, the educator will be unlikely to grow in congruence or as a teacher.

Conclusion

Teaching style is the study of matching teaching beliefs and values—the philosophy of the individual—with the behaviors used in the teaching-learning exchange. Style is a means by which we can each seek to be the best we can be in our chosen work of teaching. Perhaps most important, teaching style is the recognition that each teacher is unique, and each can use his or her style to be as effective an educator as possible.

References

Axelrod, J. "Teaching Styles in the Humanities." In W. H. Morris (ed.), *Effective College Teaching: The Quest for Relevance*. Washington, D.C.: American Council on Education, 1970.

Bem, D. J. "Self-Perception: An Alternative Interpretation of Cognitive Dissonance." *Psychological Review*, 1967, *74*, 183–200.

Brookfield, S. D. *Understanding and Facilitating Adult Learning*. San Francisco: Jossey-Bass, 1986.

Brookfield, S. D. *The Skillful Teacher: On Technique, Trust, and Responsiveness in the Classroom*. San Francisco: Jossey-Bass, 1990.

Budak, D. "The Relationship Between Teacher's Philosophy and Student Outcomes Within the Teaching-Learning Exchange in the College of Agriculture at the Ohio State University." Unpublished master's thesis, Ohio State University, 1993.

Conti, G. J. "Assessing Teaching Style in Adult Education: How and Why?" *Lifelong Learning*, 1985, *6*, 7–11, 28.

Conti, G. J. "Assessing Teaching Style in Continuing Education." In E. Hayes (ed.), *Effective Teaching Style*. New Directions for Continuing Education, no. 43. San Francisco: Jossey-Bass, 1989.

Conti, G. J. "Identifying Your Teaching Style." In M. W. Galbraith (ed.), *Adult Learning Methods: A Guide for Effective Instruction*. (2nd ed.) Malabar, Fla.: Krieger, 1998.

Cross, K. P. "Adult Learners: Characteristics, Needs and Interests." In R. E. Peterson and others (eds.), *Lifelong Learning in America*. San Francisco: Jossey-Bass, 1979.

Draves, W. A. *How to Teach Adults*. (2nd ed.) Manhattan, Kan.: Learning Resources Network, 1997.

Dunn, R. S., and Dunn, K. J. "Learning Styles/Teaching Styles: Should They . . . Can They . . . Be Matched?" *Educational Leadership*, 1979, *36*, 238–244.

Eagly, A. E., and Chaiken, S. *The Psychology of Attitudes*. Fort Worth, Tex.: Harcourt Brace, 1993.

Eble, K. E. (ed.), *Improving Teaching Styles*. New Directions for Teaching and Learning, no. 1. San Francisco: Jossey-Bass, 1980.

Fisher, B., and Fisher, L. "Styles in Teaching and Learning." *Educational Leadership*, 1979, *36*, 245–251.

Gauld, V. F. "A Study of Individual Teaching Styles of Instructors Teaching in a Non-Credit, Continuing Higher Education Program." Unpublished doctoral dissertation, University of Alabama, 1982.

Heimlich, J. E., and Meyers, R. "Method Boundness Among Zoo and Park Educators." *Environmental Education Research*, 1999, *5*, 67–75.

Heimlich, J. E., and Norland, E. *Developing Teaching Style in Adult Education*. San Francisco: Jossey-Bass, 1994.

Knowles, M. S. *The Modern Practice of Adult Education: From Pedagogy to Andragogy*. (Rev. and updated ed.) River Grove, Ill.: Follett, 1980.

Lenz, E. *The Art of Teaching Adults*. New York: Holt, 1982.

Lovell, R. B. *Adult Learning*. New York: Halsted Press, 1987.

Nuthall, G., and Snook, I. "Contemporary Models of Teaching." In R.M.W. Travers (ed.), *Second Handbook of Research on Teaching*. Skokie, Ill.: Rand McNally, 1973.

Robinson, R. D. *Helping Adults Learn and Change*. Milwaukee, Wis.: Omnibook Company, 1979.

Rokeach, M. *Beliefs, Attitudes and Values*. San Francisco: Jossey-Bass, 1968.

Seaman, D. F., and Fellenz, R. A. *Effective Strategies for Teaching Adults*. Columbus, Ohio: Merrill, 1990.

Seevers, B. S. "Factors Related to Teaching Style Preference of Ohio Cooperative Extension Faculty and Program Staff." Unpublished doctoral dissertation, Ohio State University, 1991.

Solomon, D., and Miller, H. L. *Exploration in Teaching Styles: Report of Preliminary Investigations and Development of Categories.* Chicago: Center for the Study of Liberal Education for Adults, 1961.

Tight, M. *Key Concepts in Adult Education and Training.* New York: Routledge, 2000.

Zinn, L. M. "Development of a Valid and Reliable Instrument to Identify a Personal Philosophy of Adult Education." Unpublished doctoral dissertation, Florida State University, 1983.

Zinn, L. M. "Philosophies of Education Inventory." Field test draft report, May 1994.

Zinn, L. M. "Identifying Your Philosophical Orientation." In M. W. Galbraith (ed.), *Adult Learning Methods: A Guide for Effective Instruction.* (2nd ed.) Malabar, Fla.: Krieger, 1998.

JOE E. HEIMLICH is an associate professor of environmental education in the School of Natural Resources at the Ohio State University and on temporary assignment as an associate professor in the School of Educational Policy and Leadership at the Ohio State University.

EMMALOU NORLAND is an associate professor in the School of Educational Policy and Leadership in the College of Education at the Ohio State University.

3

Teachers who make the time to prepare themselves to be mentors tend to have more satisfying and productive mentoring relationships than those who do not.

The Role of Teacher as Mentor

Lois J. Zachary

Inevitably, when I ask adults to reflect on their most significant mentoring experience, they describe a special teacher, one they say really connected with them and guided them through the memorable process of self-discovery. The learning they recall transcends a particular time and place and resulted in enduring and meaningful learning that remains useful to this day.

Teachers who prepare themselves as mentors increase their potential to enhance student growth and development, help students maximize education experiences, and enrich their own teaching experience and professional development. Mentors often report that they gain exposure to new and diverse perspectives, improve coaching and listening skills, find work more meaningful and satisfying, hone desired leadership skills, and often become reengaged professionally.

Teachers mentor students for a multitude of reasons. "As mentors, teachers typically pass on knowledge of subjects to improve educational achievement" (Heller and Sindelar, 1991, p. 7). Secondarily, teachers mentor students to facilitate personal development, encourage students to make wise choices, or help them make the transition from school to career (Zeeb, 1998).

Some teachers gravitate quite naturally toward mentoring. Others find themselves uncomfortably thrust into the role. Even under the best circumstances, most teachers are either unprepared or underprepared for the mentor role.

Whether you formally or informally mentor graduate or undergraduate adult learners, or mentor other teachers (also adult learners), adequate preparation is essential. This chapter describes the mentoring journey, provides signposts to navigate the four phases of the journey, and raises reflection questions to encourage more critically reflective mentoring practice.

New Directions for Adult and Continuing Education, no. 93, Spring 2002 © Wiley Periodicals, Inc.

The Mentoring Process

Mentoring practice has shifted from a product-oriented model, character-ized by transfer of knowledge, to a process-oriented relationship involving knowledge acquisition, application, and critical reflection. The hierarchical transfer of knowledge and information from an older, more experienced person to a younger, less experienced person is no longer the prevailing mentoring paradigm.

Learning is the fundamental process, purpose, and product of men-toring. Mentoring is best described as a reciprocal and collaborative learn-ing relationship between two or more individuals who share mutual responsibility and accountability for helping a mentee work toward achiev-ing clear and mutually defined learning goals. Commitment by and engage-ment of mentoring partners is necessary for establishing, maintaining, and experiencing successful mentoring relationships. Successful mentoring rests on building and maintaining a relationship. This means that in addi-tion to the learning, the relationship is cultivated throughout the mentor-ing partnership.

Best mentoring practice is consistent with the principles of andragogy, as articulated by Knowles (1980):

- Adults learn best when they are involved in diagnosing, planning, imple-menting, and evaluating their own learning.
- The role of the facilitator is to create and maintain a supportive climate that promotes conditions necessary for learning to take place.
- Adult learners have a need to be self-directing.
- Readiness for learning increases when there is a specific need to know.
- Life's reservoir of experience is a primary learning resource; the life expe-riences of others add enrichment to the learning process.
- Adult learners have an inherent need for immediacy of application.
- Adults respond best to learning when they are internally motivated to learn.

If mentoring relationships are to be truly learner centered, the mentor must facilitate learning by applying what is known about how adults learn to enhance the mentoring experience. According to Brookfield (1986), "Facilitators of learning see themselves as resources for learning, rather than as didactic instructors who have all the answers" (p. 63). There is an inher-ent flow to the facilitation process. A facilitator must:

- Establish a climate conducive to learning.
- Involve learners in planning how and what they will learn.
- Encourage learners to formulate their own learning objectives.
- Encourage learners to identify and utilize a variety of resources to accom-plish their objectives.
- Help learners implement and evaluate their learning [Knowles, 1980].

The strategies for promoting effective learning in a mentoring relationship are congruent with those used to facilitate student learning:

- Ask questions. The questions can open a learning conversation or shut it down.
- Reformulate statements. By rephrasing what you have heard, you clarify your own understanding and encourage the mentee to hear what it is he or she has articulated.
- Summarize. Summarizing reinforces the learning and is a reminder of what has transpired.
- Listen for the silence. Silence provides an opportunity for learning.
- Listen reflectively. When you listen reflectively, hold up a mirror for the mentee (Daloz, 1999).
- Provide consistent feedback. Candid and compassionate feedback is a powerful stimulus for learning.

The Mentoring Journey

Every mentoring journey is composed of four phases—preparing, negotiating, enabling, and coming to closure—that build on one another to form a developmental sequence and vary in length from one relationship to another (see Figure 3.1). The phases described here differ from others (Kram, 1988; Phillips-Jones, 1993; Missirian, 1982). They are less bound by time definition and psychological milestones and focus more on the behaviors required to negotiate each of the stages. And although the phases are predictable and sequential, they are not always discreet.

Awareness of each phase helps sustain successful mentoring relationships. Taking phases for granted or skipping over any can have a negative impact. Merely being aware provides significant signposts (Zachary, 2000) to stave off potentially negative consequences.

Preparing. Mentoring involves more than meeting the right teacher; the teacher must meet the right student (Palmer, 1998). To determine the right fit requires preparation of self and the mentoring relationship. Formal

Figure 3.1. Mentoring Relationship Phases

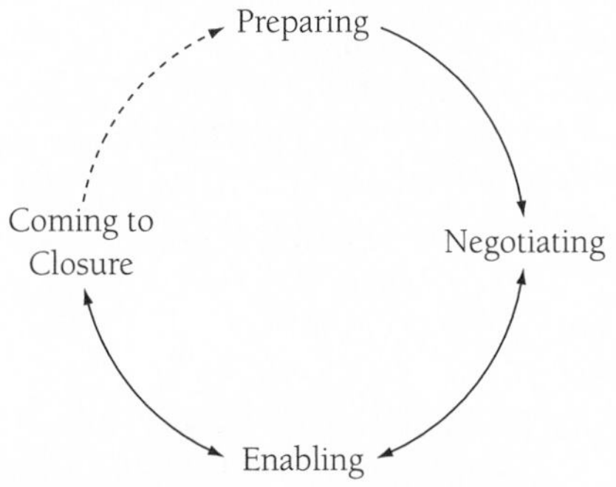

Preparing

Coming to Closure

Negotiating

Enabling

mentoring programs usually provide some assistance and training prior to assuming the role. If you are mentoring on your own, however, it is not likely that you would consider self-preparation before meeting with a prospective mentee.

Because each mentoring relationship is unique, reflective practice, which takes preparation and commitment, is the starting point. Taking the time to prepare for the relationship creates the fertile soil for embedding the mentoring relationship and adds value to the mentoring partnership.

Preparing Self. During the preparing phase of a mentoring relationship, several processes take place simultaneously. Mentors explore personal motivation and readiness to be a mentor. Individual assessment of mentoring skills helps identify areas for the mentor's learning and development. Clarity about expectation and role helps define parameters for establishing a productive and healthy mentoring relationship.

Motivation drives participation in a mentoring relationship and directly affects behavior, attitude, and emotional resilience in mentoring relationships. It also can potentially affect the quality of the mentoring interaction. Those who hold a deep understanding of why they are doing something end up being more committed to it and, because of that, focus their energy better and probably save time in the long run.

Another aspect of mentor preparation is assessing your degree of comfort with requisite mentoring skills: brokering relationships skillfully, building and maintaining relationship, coaching, communicating, encouraging, facilitating, goal setting, guiding, managing conflict, problem solving, providing, and receiving feedback and reflecting. Once you have identified areas for skill improvement, you are ready to develop a mentor development plan for yourself. Before meeting with a prospective mentoring partner you should be able to answer the following questions:

- Why do I want to be a mentor?
- Is mentoring right for me?
- Am I ready for a mentoring relationship?
- What mentoring skills do I have?
- What mentoring skills do I need?
- What are my personal development goals as a mentor?
- How will I go about enhancing my skills?

After answering these questions, you may decide that mentoring is not for you. "The complete mentor role does not fit all individuals; some faculty are less inclined toward developing close relationships with students and with nurturing the student's development. Not all faculty members are capable of or willing to take on this role, and if required to do so would be inadequate or 'incomplete' mentors" (Galbraith and Maslin-Ostrowski, 2000, p. 147).

Preparing the Relationship. The circumstances surrounding the formation of a mentoring relationship vary. Teachers may be assigned a mentee, offer to mentor a promising student, or be recruited by a student. Who does the asking is not important. The initial conversation, in which potential mentoring partners explore mutuality of interests and learning needs and determine learning fit, is critical. The outcome of this conversation helps determine if you feel you can productively work with a prospective mentee and to what extent you believe you can further this person's learning.

An initial mentoring conversation begins with making the connection— getting to know one another. You and your potential partner should talk about any past mentoring experiences. A frank discussion about relationship needs and expectations is essential. Share assumptions, expectations, and limitations candidly. In order to gauge if your experience or expertise is relevant to achieving the desired learning goals, it is necessary to take time to define desired learning outcomes. A discussion of learning styles and openness will help you identify where and if you have style compatibility.

Everyone holds assumptions about mentoring, mediated by life experiences, and these assumptions, whether we agree with them or not, influence mentoring relationships. It is essential to be aware of assumptions, whether they are institutionally or individually held. "Assumption hunting" (Brookfield, 1995) is vital to nurturing mentoring relationships. Since we all have a unique definition of what is normal in a mentoring relationship, sharing these assumptions in a disciplined way allows us to prepare for mentoring in an honest, forthright way. Sharing assumptions regarding the three terms *mentor, mentee,* and *mentoring relationships* is a revealing way to begin the assumption-hunting conversation.

An Example. A number of years ago, a student asked if I would mentor him. At first, I was intrigued by the student's initial approach, but my interest waned as we shared assumptions about what we each expected a mentor to be. In short order, it became apparent that he was looking for a mentor who was willing to "give him" all the knowledge he needed. The more we talked, the more obvious it was that he wanted to play a receiving role in his learning. He was looking for a knowledgeable, convenient mentor to deposit needed information in his head as expeditiously as possible. His preferred mode of learning made me uncomfortable. I decided instead to recommend a colleague whose style was more congruent with the student's learning style.

The Litmus Test. By the end of the initial mentoring conversation (which can extend over more than one session), both parties should know whether there is a fit and if they are prepared to move forward in the relationship. As a result, mentors should be able to answer the following questions positively:

- Am I clear about my role?
- Am I the best person for the job?
- Is this particular relationship right for me?
- Do I have the time to do justice to this relationship?

Negotiating. Negotiating is the business or contracting phase of the relationship, when mentoring partners reach agreement on learning goals and define the content and process of the relationship. During negotiating conversations, specific details of the relationship are spelled out: when and how to meet, responsibilities, criteria for success, accountability, and how and when to bring the relationship to closure. There is a natural tendency to skip over this phase of the relationship, especially by teachers, who may readily assume that this phase is superfluous.

Good conversation is essential to arriving at consensus and building commitment. "A good conversation is neither a fight nor a contest. Circular in form, cooperative in manner, and constructive in intent, it is an interchange of ideas by those who see themselves not as adversaries but as human beings coming together to talk and listen and learn from one another" (Roland Martin, 1985, p. 10). Partners engage in conversation about how the learning process will unfold and what outcomes they want to achieve during the relationship. Depth, specificity, and framework are added to the broad goals identified during the preparing phase. The outcome of this iterative phase is a partnership work plan consisting of well-defined goals, criteria and measurement for success, delineation of mutual responsibility, accountability mechanisms, and protocols for dealing with stumbling blocks.

An Example. From my first contact with Mark, it was apparent that he needed considerable support to complete each assignment. He needed a specific detailed itemization of what was required and a model for him to follow. My role as a teacher was to provide a compass, not a road map, since this was, after all, a graduate-level course. As I provided feedback, his confidence grew. But his writing skills were weak, and so I gently but firmly helped him realize that he was going to need help if he intended to complete his academic program successfully. Toward the end of the course, he approached me and asked me if I would mentor him through the writing process. After our initial conversation, I agreed. I asked him to bring his completed writing assignments to the next session, and we reviewed them together.

We used the learnings to define what he wanted to accomplish and discussed his self-imposed deadline. I already knew about his weak learning style and that he was going to stick to a concrete and specific schedule that had clear tasks and deadlines built into it. We spent time talking about accountability and feedback. I let him know that some of what he would be hearing might be hard to accept and that if he wanted to develop his writing, he was going to need to listen not only to his own voice but to some critical feedback. He was also going to have to shoulder the responsibility because no external accountability was being placed on him.

The real value of negotiating conversations like this one lies in the conversation process that creates the shared understanding or working agreements about some of the soft issues in a relationship—topics like confidentiality, boundaries, and limits, which are often omitted in mentoring conversations because they are uncomfortable or difficult to talk about. Although some individuals fear that such a discussion undermines trust, it in fact lays a solid foundation for building trust.

The Litmus Test. By the end of the negotiating conversation, which may take one or more sessions, you should be able to answer the following questions:

- What are the learner's goals?
- What are the learner's needs?
- Is there mutual understanding of roles?
- What are the responsibilities of each partner?
- What are the norms of the relationship?
- How often should we meet?
- How often should we connect?
- What is our agreement?
- What are our operating assumptions about confidentiality?
- What are the boundaries and limits of this relationship?
- What is our work plan?
- How and when will the relationship be brought to closure?
- What are our criteria for success?

When you can address all of these questions, you are ready to move on to the enabling phase and implement the mentoring partnership agreement.

Enabling. The enabling phase takes longer to complete than other mentoring phases, for this is when the greatest learning between mentoring partners takes place. Although it offers opportunity for nurturing learning and development, it is also when mentoring partners are most vulnerable to obstacles that may derail the relationship.

Each mentoring relationship is unique and must find its own path. Although goals are clearly articulated, the process is well defined, and the milestones are identified, path finding takes time. The learning that takes place during the enabling phase depends on maintaining a climate of mutual trust and respect.

The mentor's role during this phase is to nurture mentee growth by maintaining an open and affirming learning climate, asking the right questions at the right time, and providing thoughtful, timely, candid, and constructive feedback (Zachary, 2000). The learning progress and the learning process should be continuously monitored to ensure that the mentee's learning goals are being met. Learning milestones should be acknowledged and celebrated.

An Example. I had been assigned the task of mentoring a new faculty member. The learning goals of our relationship had been established by our institution, and because we shared a history as colleagues, the preparing stage was a relatively short one. We checked out our assumptions in the negotiating phase and spent time talking about learning styles. We agreed on a process to complement her learning style. We decided to begin with some articles and materials that would provide her with a baseline orientation. She would do some shadowing, and we would build in regular conversation time to answer questions as they arose. We decided to attend the new faculty orientation program together and review each session at the end of the day. We looked at past student papers, which illustrated the sort of feedback I have given students, and we even met with some students together. She was eager to get started and met with some students herself. Each experience raised additional questions for her. For a while, she asked me to read some student evaluations she had drafted. When she was ready, she began her work in earnest, confident that she was well prepared.

What I was endeavoring to do was to provide adequate support, appropriate challenge, and ample vision (Daloz, 1999) to facilitate her learning throughout the enabling phase. I was able to manage the relationship and support her learning by creating a climate for learning. Her continuous feedback made me keenly aware that the level of support she required was not the same support I needed when I was being oriented to that role. I was able to maintain the momentum by providing challenge at the appropriate level (when the challenge was too great, my mentee so informed me) and monitoring the process and evaluating progress. I encouraged her development in the role by providing vision. I served as a guide, provided the map, and held up a mirror to foster reflection and encourage her as she was working hard to achieve the desired learning outcomes. Table 3.1 illustrates how Daloz's (1999) conditions of support, challenge, and vision relate to the ongoing work of this phase.

The Litmus Test. Mentors ensure the integrity of the process when they take time during the enabling phase to reflect on the following questions:

- Have we established a regular pattern of conduct?
- How well are we communicating with one another?
- What kinds of development opportunities am I providing to support fulfillment of my mentee's goals?
- How can I improve the quality of the mentoring interaction?
- Are we continuing to work at maintaining the trust in this relationship?
- Am I providing thoughtful, candid, and constructive feedback?
- Is my mentee using the feedback to take action?
- Are there some lurking dangers or undiscussable issues (that is, things not talked about, perhaps because of discomfort on the part of the mentor or mentee to do so) in the mentoring relationship?
- What additional learning opportunities, resources, and venues should we add to enhance the learning experience?
- Are we taking time to reflect on our partnership regularly?
- Is the quality of our mentoring interaction satisfactory?

Coming to Closure. Coming to closure is an evolutionary process, which actually starts in the negotiating phase when mentoring partners establish closure procedures. As partners get to know each other during the enabling phase, they become more aware of each other's interests and needs, and they are in a better position to plan closure collaboratively. During the coming to closure phase, mentoring partners implement their exit strategy,

Table 3.1. Nurturing Growth in the Enabling Phase

Conditions That Facilitate Growth and Development[a]	Enabling Process and Functions[b]	Mentor's Key Tasks
Support	Managing the Process Listening Providing structure Expressing positive expectations Serving as advocate Sharing ourselves Making it special	• Creating a learning environment • Building and maintaining the relationship
Challenge	Maintaining Momentum Setting tasks Engaging in discussion Setting up dichotomies Constructing hypotheses Setting high standards	• Monitoring the process • Evaluating progress
Vision	Encouraging Movement Modeling Keeping tradition Offering a map Suggesting new language Providing a mirror	• Fostering reflection • Assessing learning outcomes

Source: The Mentor's Guide, Lois J. Zachary, Copyright © 2000, Jossey-Bass Publishers. Reprinted by permission of Jossey-Bass, Inc., a subsidiary of John Wiley and Sons, Inc.
[a]See Daloz (1999, Chap. 8) for full description of the facilitative behaviors.
[b]The functions listed in Column 2 are discussed extensively in Daloz (1999) and are not directly explained in this chapter. They are listed here to illustrate the processes a mentor might use to enable mentee learning.

ensuring that there is a learning conclusion, no matter what the circumstances (Zachary, 2000).

This seemingly short phase offers a rich opportunity for growth and reflection regardless of whether the relationship has been positive. Coming to closure presents a developmental opportunity for mentors and mentees to harvest their learning and move on.

Closure encompasses evaluating the learning, acknowledging progress, and celebrating achievement of the learning. Mentors, as well as mentees, benefit from closure. When closure is seen as an opportunity to evaluate personal learning and take that learning to the next level, mentors leverage their own learning and growth.

Coming to closure presents a serious challenge for mentoring partners. The reasons are legion. Anxiety, resentment, or surprise can sabotage the closure experience. It is difficult to plan for closure because relationships can end earlier or last longer than anticipated. Sometimes partners cannot let a mentoring relationship end because of the emotions and personal ties inherent in any relationship. Sometimes inertia or a sense of comfort sustains a mentoring relationship long after the relationship should have ended.

Some mentoring partnerships end with successful completion of learning goals. Some do not. Even unproductive or unsatisfactory mentoring relationships benefit from a positive closure experience. If closure is to be a mutually satisfying learning experience, mentoring partners must be prepared with an exit strategy. A good exit strategy has four components:

1. A learning conclusion (reflection on learning outcomes) and process for integrating what was learned (how to apply the learning and taking it to the next level)
2. A meaningful way to celebrate success (collaboratively planning a mutually satisfying way to celebrate)
3. A conversation focusing on redefining the relationship (talking about how the relationship is to continue; whether it moves from professional mentoring relationship to colleague, friendship, or ceases to exist at all)
4. A comfortable way of moving on (acknowledging transition and identifying ways to sever the relationship or stay in contact)

An Example. I recently mentored a student who was studying the topic of mentoring adolescent girls. We talked about closure during the second session and agreed at that time that we both wanted a positive closure experience, even if the relationship did not work out. We agreed that we did not know each other well enough to know what appropriate closure might be and decided to revisit the closure process midway through our mentoring contract. When we did, we tossed around ideas, but neither of us was particularly enamoured with any of the options. We learned shortly thereafter that Marian Wright Edelman was speaking at a local event and decided that attending the event together would be particularly meaningful. As we sat together at the event, we talked about the process we had been through and acknowledged particularly meaningful learnings. We also shared our appreciation of each other. Attending the event was special, and being there together was especially significant.

The Litmus Test. The completion of learning goals signals the time for closure of the relationship. Prior to bringing the relationship to closure, mentors should consider the following questions:

- What are the signals that indicate now is time for closure?
- Have we established closure protocols?
- How are we going to acknowledge and celebrate accomplishments?
- What are the learning outcomes of this relationship for me and for my mentee?
- How am I going to apply what I have learned from this relationship?

- In what ways can I help my mentee think about taking her learning to the next level?
- Where does the relationship go from here?

Lessons Learned

Teaching and mentoring both focus on the work of facilitating learning. Being successful in the teacher role does not guarantee mentoring success; however, good teaching practice does inform good mentoring, and vice versa. Palmer (1990) reminds us that "good teachers dwell in the mystery of good teaching until it dwells in them. As they explore it alone and with others, the insight and energy of mystery begins to inform and animate their work" (p. 11).

As we engage in mentoring, we bring our own cycle, our own timetable, our own history, our own individuality, and our own ways of doing things to each relationship. For learning to occur, we must understand who we are, what we bring, and what our mentoring partner brings to the relationship. We must also understand the complexity of the mentoring relationship. We must understand the ebb and flow of the learning process. In sum, we must prepare ourselves to meet the challenge so that our efforts can have profound, deep, and enduring impact on our students. Being part of a mentoring partnership involves conscious choice and challenges each of us to think about what we might become and to remember Ralph Waldo Emerson's sage words, "What lies behind and lies before us are small matters to what lies within us."

References

Brookfield, S. D. *Understanding and Facilitating Adult Learning.* San Francisco: Jossey-Bass, 1986.

Brookfield, S. D. *Becoming a Critically Reflective Teacher.* San Francisco: Jossey-Bass, 1995.

Daloz, L. *Mentor: Guiding the Journey of Adult Learners.* San Francisco: Jossey-Bass, 1999.

Galbraith, M. W., and Maslin-Ostrowski, P. "The Mentor Facilitating Out-of-Class Cognitive and Affective Growth." In J. L. Bess and others (eds.), *Teaching Alone, Teaching Together: Transforming the Structure of Teams for Teaching.* San Francisco: Jossey-Bass, 2000.

Heller, M. P., and Sindelar, N. W. *Developing an Effective Teacher Mentor Program.* Bloomington, Ind.: Phi Delta Kappa Educational Foundation, 1991. (ED 332 996)

Knowles, M. S. *The Modern Practice of Adult Education: From Pedagogy to Andragogy.* (Rev. and updated ed.) River Grove, Ill.: Follett, 1980.

Kram, K. E. *Mentoring at Work: Developmental Relationships in Organizational Life.* Glenview, Ill.: Scott, Foresman, 1988.

Missirian, A. K. *The Corporate Connection: Why Executive Women Need Mentors to Reach the Top.* Upper Saddle River, N.J.: Prentice Hall, 1982.

Palmer, P. J. "Good Teaching: A Matter of Living the Mystery." *Change,* 1990, 22, 11–16.

Palmer, P. J. *The Courage to Teach.* San Francisco: Jossey-Bass, 1998.

Phillips-Jones, L. *The New Mentors and Protégés.* Cypress Valley, Calif.: Coalition of Counseling Centers, 1993.

Roland Martin, J. *Reclaiming a Conversation: The Ideal of the Educated Woman.* New Haven, Conn.: Yale University Press, 1985.

Zachary, L. *The Mentor's Guide: Facilitating Effective Learning Relationships.* San Francisco: Jossey-Bass, 2000.

Zeeb, P. A. *Teaching Through Mentoring.* Richmond: Virginia Commonwealth University. [http://coe.sdus.edu/et640/popsamples/pzeeb/pzeeb.htm.] 1998.

LOIS J. ZACHARY is president of Leadership Development Services, LLC, a consulting firm in Phoenix, Arizona.

4

Race is a variable that affects the teaching and learning transaction both overtly and covertly.

Race Matters: The Unspoken Variable in the Teaching-Learning Transaction

Juanita Johnson-Bailey

Adult education is a reflection of the society in which we live. It exhibits our values, reproduces existing systems of power, and functions to maintain the status quo. In these ways, it is similar to all other levels of education in Western society in that it is based on a hierarchical system where privilege is usually accorded along existing lines of established rights and entitlement. Adult education, which was conceived as a field in the early twentieth century, was embedded with a charge from its major theorists and by its epistemological processes to work toward full citizenship and the democratization of the entire adult populace (Cunningham, 1988).

Despite the stated good intentions of the field, adult education has not succeeded in accomplishing the lofty goals of empowering those lacking basic skills and in bringing all citizens to the table of equal access and opportunity. Indeed, the barriers that have crippled the field's goals, including race, class, gender, ethnicity, disability, and sexual orientation, continue to divide and disable society in general. How are these issues manifest in the delivery of adult education services? There are many avenues through which societal issues enter adult education practices: however, programs and class curricula, student enrollment, student interactions, and faculty makeup are the most apparent foci in any discussion of how the adult education system operates. As educators, how can we best grapple with the dilemma of who we are serving, and how can we foster a teaching and learning environment of equity and empowerment? I believe the answer for practitioners lies in day-to-day teaching and learning transactions.

Race in Adult Education

Many variables drive the teaching and learning transaction. This chapter examines one of these issues: race. My intention by this choice is not to suggest that race is the most significant or important of the variables. Because power operates in similar ways to disenfranchise women, people of color, gays, and the disabled, race is therefore offered as a salient and representative constant that can be used as an instrument with which to make comparisons and evaluations.

In examining race, it is necessary to establish a working definition that is applicable to American society. Race is a social construct (Gregory and Sanjek, 1994; Winant, 1994) used to organize people into groups according to their physical appearance. In addition, racial clustering encompasses tacit ideas concerning the intellectual, physical, and moral tenets of group members. Although scientists agree that definitive racial codification is based on a nebulous set of physical characteristics, such classification systems stand as primary ways in which we identify people in Western society. Admittedly, no matter how ambiguous racial classification may be, race profoundly affects how a person functions in this society (Giroux, 1997; McIntosh, 1995). Therefore to be Asian, African American, Hispanic, Native American, or White in the adult education classroom carries a different meaning with each classification. Yet in the field of adult education, we frequently ignore these arbitrary distinctions by proceeding with generic praxis, literature, and discourses.

The notion of the adult education classroom as a neutral territory where a facilitator functions to bring all participants into a shared dialogue is the archetype set forth in the literature (Apps, 1991; Brookfield, 1995; Knowles, 1992). The fact that our classrooms are the real world, with preset hierarchical power relations, remains largely unacknowledged. When we participate in programs or classes as students, instructors, or planners, we bring the historical weight of race with us. It matters little whether we intentionally trade on or naively try to discard the privileges, the deficits, or standpoints of racial statuses. Such ranks, authorizations, honors, suspicions, and stereotypes cannot be cast aside. They are accrued in society's invisible hierarchical banking system of trading and bartering according to designated racial rankings. If teachers are to function proficiently, they must acknowledge and manage the uninvited specters of race that haunt our practices.

The Importance of Discussing Race

In general, speaking of race in the United States means speaking of people of color. One major marker of disenfranchisement in Western civilization is race: people of color are disproportionately poor and locked out of full participation. The group designated as minority varies according to the critical mass in a geographical area. For instance, when educators in Texas talk about minority concerns, the minority in question are Mexicanas(nos), and in Oklahoma they are referring to Native Americans. As a hierarchical society, we rank-order groups according to their alleged contributions and participation in maintaining society. We value one group over another in terms of tax dollars generated and in turn allocate that group greater or fewer resources to support basic needs, including education. The implicit understanding that those who have more in a capitalistic order will receive more translates directly into how educational dollars will be disbursed. Many studies have well documented that in the United States, disenfranchised groups routinely receive substandard K-12 educations and have less access to higher and adult education. For disenfranchised adult learners, the consequences of a system that parcels out educational benefits based on privilege can be demonstrated in several ways. For instance, such systemic practices could result in libraries, community centers, and community colleges being built in areas that are not proximate to their communities. And so for minority learners, their race can affect the quality of their education well beyond the boundaries of tax-based mandatory education and intrude into the realms of voluntary client-sponsored adult education.

Despite the importance of race to educational access, disenfranchisement and enfranchisement as related to education and group membership are rarely discussed in tandem. When the poor and undereducated are the center of the discourse, what is absent in discussions is the norm of enfranchised learners and privileged students who remain the measure of comparisons. Researchers often present data on one group and represent the other group in silent absentia. However, in order for any discussion on adult education to be complete, the examination must not only give statistics on who participates, how they are instructed, and how they learn but must also include who does not participate or who seldom participates, how they are instructed, and how they learn.

Research on teaching and learning in adult education acknowledges the delicate dance between teaching and learning but does not extend the conversation by examining the possible interconnectivity. Brookfield (1986) states of the teaching-learning transaction, "It is a highly complex psychosocial drama in which the personalities of the individual involved, the contextual setting for the educational transaction, and the prevailing political climate crucially affect the nature and form of learning" (p. vii). Yet missing from the complexities that Brookfield and others have explored is the enigmatic nature of race in American society as an important part of this "psychosocial drama."

Perspectives on Race in Adult Education Literature

Although educators and practitioners acknowledge race as a variable that affects teaching and learning, they do so without fully acknowledging how race shapes the ways in which we plan and practice. We frequently use terms like *underprivileged students, at-risk learners,* and *minority students* to identify and label certain populations. However, we do not expand our thinking to understand how the life conditions of underprivileged learners play out in their everyday classroom circumstances. How do such learners fare in classrooms and programs? How does our thinking about these learners affect our practice and our field?

The way we think invariably affects the way we research, write, and teach. A survey of the literature by Cafferella and Olson (1993) indicates that the majority of the field's major studies do not incorporate gender or race as factors in the sample population. An examination of race in the major adult education textbooks (Johnson-Bailey and Cervero, 2000) used throughout the field reveals the same lack of attention to race as a variable. The literature surveyed shows that three major outlooks or stances are routinely used regarding race: the color-blind, multicultural, and social justice perspectives (Johnson-Bailey, 2000). Each view affects research and praxis.

Color-Blind Perspective. A survey of adult education literature will not reveal a position labeled as the color-blind outlook. However, this term seems well suited to a stance that does not acknowledge race or that views all racial issues as inconsequential when not expressed as part of any classroom or curriculum equation. This attitude, which remains oblivious to difference, is the most widely used approach among adult educators. Overall, race is either not mentioned or is rarely discussed in the adult education textbooks (Johnson-Bailey and Cervero, 2000). In a major survey of adult education graduate program curricula, race was conspicuously absent, with the exception being courses on cultural diversity or community education (Milton, Watkins, Spears-Studdard, and Burch, 2001).

In the major philosophies and concepts that drive the field, such as andragogy (Knowles, 1980), the notion of race and the way it affects learners is not considered. From Knowles's standpoint, climate setting more directly involves other attributes, such as the physical environment. Knowles and his proponents do not recognize that the educational environment is not a neutral setting and that some learners enter the classroom in deficit positions that have been imposed by society. A clear example of how commonplace adult education practices discount race as a factor is seen in the use of small group activity. The traditional adult education practice rests on the notion that all learners will feel comfortable with their co-learners and will therefore share ideas and opinions. However, not all learners, especially Latinas and Native Americans, are enculturated to speak as individuals; rather, they are culturally grounded to consider the group as more important than the individual. In many Asian cultures, speaking out is seen as seeking individual honor and is assessed as shameful behavior. In addition, Knowles and his supporters naively assume that all participants will treat each other with respect and that differences or struggles based on racial tensions will not enter into classroom dynamics.

Multicultural or Cultural Diversity Perspective. The second view that is manifest in adult education is the multicultural or cultural diversity perspective. This position sets forth that society comprises different cultures that imbue their members with values, folkways, and mores and that one's experiences can be significantly influenced by one's cultural membership. Furthermore, multiculturalism calls for the recognition of the accomplishments of each culture and sees this acceptance as a way of valuing each group and as a step toward bringing equity to the educational setting and potentially to the larger society. This perspective has found widespread acceptance, especially in the light of globalization as an emerging research area in the adult education component of human resource development.

An example of how the field accesses the contributions of disenfranchised groups is readily evident in the add-difference-and-stir approach, as seen in most adult education textbooks published in the past decade. This method refers to the way authors trivialize the significance of race in their authored or edited texts and sourcebooks by adding on a final chapter that pertains to minority concerns. These chapters are usually offered to placate the concerns of politically conscious publishers or readers to whom they would not want to be appear exclusionary.

Social Justice Perspective. The third outlook takes a moral position that critiques society as unjust toward minorities and other disenfranchised groups and calls for the field to remember its mission to work toward democratization. Although this message has been present since the field's inception, it is experiencing a resurgence in direct response to the prolific writings of Afrocentric and feminist adult education scholars (Guy, 1999; Hart, 1985; Hayes and Flannery, 2000; Sheared and Sissel, 2000; Tisdell, 1995). The focus of this position is twofold: to highlight the moral imperative and commitment of adult education and to work to empower adult learners. Focusing on the workings of power as a force that drives society and the classroom, social justice advocates urge practitioners to examine the embedded privilege in classroom practices and the curriculum.

According to Cunningham (1996), if we are not working for equity in our teaching and learning environments, then adult educators are inadvertently maintaining the status quo. Other supporters (Rocco and West, 1998; Tisdell, 1995) write specifically about dialogue and the use of voice as analogous to how power and privilege are manifested in routine classroom workings: students who feel powerful and validated by the teacher or the curriculum talk, and students who feel neglected or ignored by the teacher or the curriculum remain silent. Rocco and West (1998) and Tisdell (1995) also cite race as a major location of power and privilege in society and in adult education classrooms.

How Positionality Drives the Teaching and Learning Transaction

Overall, in adult education, teaching and learning has existed as a generic concept for the past fifty years: all teachers and learners are the same (Brown, 1997). In the 1990s, several adult education scholars turned their attention to how power affects teaching and learning (Collard and Stalker,

1991; Johnson-Bailey and Cervero, 1997, 1998; Rocco and West, 1998; Sheared, 1994; Tisdell, 1993). In one study, Tisdell (1993) notes that the power dynamics that exist in the classroom between instructors and learners and between learners and their co-learners are often affected by gender and racial differences. Sheared (1994) posits that teachers and students will have varying sets of experiences that will be determined by their race, economic status, and language skills, as well as their personal experiences.

Subsequent studies conducted in adult settings have shown that both teaching and learning are affected by the race of the participants (Brown, 1997; Johnson-Bailey and Cervero, 1998). Brown (1997) found that women of color who taught math to adults in community college and other higher education settings offered narratives and supporting documentation to show that they were perceived differently from their White counterparts. The data showed that often the students challenged the Black math teachers' knowledge base, openly consulted other math teachers to check their expertise, and reported alleged teacher infractions to a supervisor.

In a separate study, Johnson-Bailey and Cervero (1998) noted similar concerns. However, their study, which focused on the influences of race on teaching and learning, used both the teachers and the students as units of analysis. The comparative case study examined two graduate courses taught by adult education professors: one White male professor and one Black female assistant professor. Using Maher and Tetreault's (1994) four themes—mastery, voice, authority, and positionality—as organizing concepts, the researchers used student evaluations, teacher observation, student and teacher interviews, syllabi, and peer debriefing as data sources. Allowing for issues of faculty rank and gender, the data indicated that the race of the teachers affected the message received by the students and the class interactions between the instructors and students and between students and their classmates. Although the White male professor had race as a central class topic, the learners never perceived him as pressing an agenda. In addition, they never questioned his competence, fairness, and classroom management. The Black female professor, who did not have race as a central topic, was seen as having an agenda that overtly supported racial equity. Incidents that both the female professor and the students reported showed that the learners carefully scrutinized her competence, fairness, and classroom management and saw her race as "the most salient issue" (Johnson-Bailey & Cervero, 1998, p. 396).

Other important findings in this study have particular implications for adult educators. Analysis revealed that White male students experienced a high degree of comfort when they were free to talk without being checked and when they were called on to serve as group leaders. In environments where power issues were not regulated by the instructor, the White males were permitted to claim their culturally ascribed power roles of leadership. Conversely, disenfranchised learners were direct in expressing how uncomfortable they were in a classroom setting where power dynamics were not controlled by the teacher. However, they reported a significant level of comfort when they were allowed voice and felt that the instructor valued their opinions. For example, in this same study, Black learners felt that they were allowed to thrive when the teacher monitored who talked in class and ensured that there was ample communication space for all students.

In summary, the literature shows that learning environments are not neutral sites; they are instead driven in large part by the positionalities of the instructors and learners, with a conspicuous component of the makeup being race. Race is seen as a critical lens for assessing classroom teaching and learning experiences. The dimension is multifaceted; the race of both the instructor and the students drives the dynamic of interactions that take place in a teaching-learning environment.

Practical Views on Race and the Teaching-Learning Transaction

A tension exists in the field of adult education between "technical competency and informed practical action" (Wilson and Hayes, 2000, p. 25) and theory and experiential intuitive practice. Nowhere is that more evident than in the teaching and delivery of programs and classes to adults. Brookfield has long offered critical reflection as the answer to this dilemma. Yet on a tenuous note, Brookfield (2000) cautions that a practitioner's experiential base can limit or affect the way he or she assesses his or her practices when they include power into the concept of critical reflection:

> We realize that in order to do good work we must consistently involve others—particularly learners and colleagues—as commentators on our efforts. In a very real sense we depend on these people to keep us honest. When we come to a position as educators of constantly soliciting learners' perceptions, and of negotiating and reframing what we do on the basis of these, it seems to me we are practicing more, rather than less, democratically. When we elevate learners' voices to a position of prominence we are working in an inclusive and collaborative way [p. 47].

Brookfield ends his charge by saying that educators and practitioners should be mindful of learners' experiences and opinions and intimates the individual nature of the learner. Yet he neglects to make direct reference to collective issues that commonly silence the voices of entire racial groups.

Adult education's current embrace of critical reflection is a promising direction. Critical reflection is flexible enough to serve the field well and also to open avenues for negotiating issues of diversity and difference. Although teaching cannot be reduced to a paint-by-numbers task, it often seems to be portrayed as such since the literature overwhelmingly presents the art and science of teaching as an area that can be mastered if practitioners follow the prescriptive and descriptive means provided. Critical reflection allows for the use of prescriptive or descriptive discourses but nevertheless provides the codicil that one's teaching practice is always evolving, with growth and maturity dependent on a rigor achieved through personal assessment and input from all stakeholders.

As practitioners, we must reflect on how race affects our teaching environments and how we manage these intersections. Practitioners can incorporate three options into their critical reflection to guide them in auditing their teaching-learning transactions: (1) a personal appraisal and understanding of their own cultural history, (2) a functional grasp of the sociopolitical forces that affect the learners and the learning environment, and (3) an evaluation of whether their own practice is part of the solution or part of the problem.

First, as a woman of color teaching in an adult education graduate program and researching and writing about race and gender, I can easily lose sight of my own privilege: I have a terminal degree; I am tenured; I am able-bodied; I am a married heterosexual; I am middle class; I am Catholic. Although my research critiques the hegemonic relations between the powerful and the powerless, I am not compelled to reside with the powerless on the margins in reality or in abstraction. Despite the overall disenfranchisement of people of my race, I generally find shelter in an inner circle that allows my accomplishments to mitigate any commonly held racial stereotypes about my group. In an effort to reconcile my academic place of comfort with my real-world position, I frequently revisit the variances of my background. Banks (1994) calls this process conducting a cultural therapy exercise to consider how one's culture affects the teaching-learning exchange. This method of critical reflection keeps the positionality of race—mine and my learners'—in an integral position. In addition, privilege is cast as a context-dependent force rather than depicting Whiteness and maleness as possessing the permanent high ground of rights and entitlements.

Second, as a practitioner in a diverse adult education graduate program, I am still surprised at the silence I encounter in the classroom from African Americans, Asians, and the occasional Latino student. Speaking out and being heard is a right that is assumed by Whites, and particularly White males in our society. Being taught to stay silent and thereby finding acceptance is a traditional coping mechanism that minorities use in educational settings (Johnson-Bailey, 2001). Yet silence as a response from disenfranchised students is often accepted without question by practitioners and is rarely deconstructed as problematic to teaching and learning. The socialized issue of silence or lack of voice bears investigation and mediation. The instructor can provide alternative means of communicating, such as through journals or one-page reaction papers or through solicited responses from students of color who do not freely participate in classroom exchanges. Modeling behavior that emphasizes give-and-take in dialogue is another method of fostering a respectful classroom space.

One recommendation is that instructors observe the setting to monitor not only who speaks but also who interacts with whom and who takes a leadership role in small group work as part of effective teaching. This is an important way of accessing the power dynamics in the classroom. Often an instructor needs to negotiate classroom conversations and debates, as well as regulate student networks and small group activities, to ensure that these exchanges contribute to a democratic classroom environment. Such monitoring is essential because what happens between and among students affects the quality of teaching, as well as the caliber of the learning.

Another factor that profoundly affects the classroom group strategies that we commonly use as adult educators is the individuation within groups and between groups. Typically in Western society, we live within our own enclaves, unfamiliar with people of different races, religions, and cultures. A lack of familiarity with different racial groups is common in the adult education classroom given our American legacy: a country that was legally segregated until the mid-1950s and divided by convention until the 1970s, and today remains segmented by custom into racial and cultural groups. This history can significantly affect both the teaching and learning experience. Adult educators need to remain cognizant of this variable. Often it is necessary to navigate this maze of unfamiliarity through assigned readings, controlling the mix of small groups, and discussing possible barriers with students.

Finally, the struggle to promote equity in the learning environment through the way we teach or facilitate is ongoing. No matter how far one travels, one never reaches a final destination of establishing a teaching and learning space that is safe and fair. As bell hooks (1989) reminds us, power continuously co-opts. Therefore being satisfied with one's practice sanctions a sense of false comfort. Being a person of color or an empathetic majority member does not provide an automatic understanding or offer solutions for managing a racially diverse setting in such a way that race is never an impediment to the exchange of knowledge. When practitioners no longer struggle to find texts that include different voices and views, when they fail to establish a curriculum that is inclusive and responsive to diversity, or when they do not challenge research that accepts the hegemonic influence of the culture, then they must assuredly be part of the problem.

Does Race Matter?

A glance at the diversity of our world versus the roster of our programs and classrooms, which do not reflect proportional diversity, suggests that race does indeed matter. In what ways does teaching reproduce a setting where learners are not equally valued? One explanation to this dilemma lies in understanding how we teach and represent ourselves and our discipline.

Among the questions that we can routinely ask to evaluate how we conduct our practice and manage our programs are these:

- Are the numbers of students of color growing?
- Do students of color routinely take my classes?
- Is the talk in my class a balanced exchange?
- Is there a healthy and inclusive network in my program or class?
- Is there a vigorous and tense exchange of ideas?

If the responses to these questions are fleeting, then perhaps our teaching and learning transactions in adult education are not appropriately responsive to issues of race as an essential force in our hierarchical world.

References

Apps, J. *Mastering the Teaching of Adults.* Malabar, Fla.: Krieger, 1991.

Banks, J. A. *An Introduction to Multicultural Education.* Needham Heights, Mass.: Allyn & Bacon, 1994.

Brookfield, S. D. *Understanding and Facilitating Adult Learning.* San Francisco: Jossey-Bass, 1986.

Brookfield, S. D. *Becoming a Critically Reflective Teacher.* San Francisco: Jossey-Bass, 1995.

Brookfield, S. D. "The Concept of Critically Reflective Practice." In A. L. Wilson and E. R. Hayes (eds.), *Handbook of Adult and Continuing Education.* San Francisco: Jossey-Bass, 2000.

Brown, A. "Making the Invisible Visible by Challenging the Myth of the Universal Teacher: African American Women Post-Secondary Mathematics Teachers." Unpublished doctoral dissertation, University of Georgia, 1997.

Caffarella, R. S., and Olson, S. K. "Psychosocial Development of Women: A Critical Review of the Literature." *Adult Education Quarterly,* 1993, *43,* 125–151.

Collard, S., and Stalker, J. "Women's Trouble: Women, Gender, and the Learning Environment." In R. Hiemstra (ed.), *Creating Environments for Effective Adult Learning.* San Francisco: Jossey-Bass, 1991.

Cunningham, P. M. "The Adult Educator and Social Responsibility." In R. G. Brockett (ed.), *Ethical Issues in Adult Education.* New York: Teachers College Press, 1988.

Cunningham, P. M. "Race, Gender, Class, and the Practice of Adult Education in the United States." In P. Wangoola and F. Youngman (eds.), *Towards a Transformative Political Economy of Adult Education: Theoretical and Practical Challenges.* DeKalb, Ill.: LEPS Press, 1996.

Giroux, H. A. "Rewriting the Discourse of Racial Identity: Towards a Pedagogy and Politics of Whiteness." *Harvard Educational Review,* 1997, *67,* 285–320.

Gregory, S., and Sanjek, R. (eds.). *Race.* New Brunswick, N.J.: Rutgers University Press, 1994.

Guy, T. "Culturally Relevant Instruction for African American Adults: African American English (AAE) as an Instructional Resource for Teachers of African American Adults." In D. Ntiri (ed.), *Instructional Strategies to Enhance Adult Learning.* Detroit: Wayne State University, 1999.

Hart, M. "Thematization of Power, the Search for Common Interest, and Self-Reflection: Towards a Comprehensive Concept of Emancipatory Education." *International Journal of Lifelong Education,* 1985, *4,* 119–134.

Hayes, E., and Flannery, D. D. *Women as Learners: The Significance of Gender in Adult Learning.* San Francisco: Jossey-Bass, 2000.

hooks, b. *Talking Back: Thinking Feminist, Thinking Black.* Boston: South End Press, 1989.

Johnson-Bailey, J. *Sistahs in College: Making a Way Out of No Way.* Malabar, Fla.: Krieger, 2001.

Johnson-Bailey, J., and Cervero, R. M. "Negotiating Power Dynamics in Workshops." In J. Fleming (ed.), *New Perspectives on Designing and Implementing Effective Workshops.* New Directions for Adult and Continuing Education, no. 76. San Francisco: Jossey-Bass, 1997.

Johnson-Bailey, J., and Cervero, R. M. "Power Dynamics in Teaching and Learning Practices: An Examination of Two Adult Education Classrooms." *International Journal of Lifelong Education*, 1998, 17, 389–399.

Johnson-Bailey, J., and Cervero, R. M. "The Invisible Politics of Race in Adult Education." In A. L. Wilson and E. R. Hayes (eds.), *Handbook of Adult and Continuing Education.* San Francisco: Jossey-Bass, 2000.

Knowles, M. S. *The Modern Practice of Adult Education: From Pedagogy to Andragogy.* (Rev. and updated ed.) River Grove, Ill.: Follett, 1980.

Knowles, M. *The Adult Learner: A Neglected Species.* (4th ed.) Houston: Gulf, 1992.

Maher, F., and Tetreault, M. *The Feminist Classroom.* New York: Basic Books, 1994.

McIntosh, P. "White Privilege and Male Privilege: A Personal Accounting of Coming to See Correspondences Through Work in Women's Studies." In M. L. Anderson and P. H. Collins (eds.), *Race, Class, and Gender.* Belmont, Calif.: Wadsworth, 1995.

Merriam, S. B. *Qualitative Research and Case Study Applications in Education.* San Francisco: Jossey-Bass, 1998.

Milton, J., Watkins, K., Spears-Studdard, S., and Burch, M. "An Ever Widening Gyre: Factors Affecting Change in Adult Education Graduate Programs." Unpublished manuscript, 2001.

Rocco, T., and West, G. "Deconstructing Privilege: An Examination of Privilege in Adult Education." *Adult Education Quarterly*, 1998, 48, 171–184.

Sheared, V. "Giving Voice: An Inclusive Model of Instruction—A Womanist Perspective." In E. Hayes and S. Colin (eds.), *Confronting Racism and Sexism.* San Francisco: Jossey-Bass, 1994.

Sheared, V., and Sissel, P. *Making Space: Merging Theory to Practice in Adult Education.* Westport, Conn.: Greenwood Press, 2000.

Tisdell, E. "Interlocking Systems of Power, Privilege, and Oppression in Adult Higher Education Classes." *Adult Education Quarterly*, 1993, 3, 203–226.

Tisdell, E. *Creating Inclusive Adult Learning Environments: Insights from Multicultural and Feminist Pedagogy.* Columbus, Ohio: ERIC Clearinghouse on Adult, Career, and Vocational Education, 1995.

Wilson, A. L., and Hayes, E. R. (eds.). *Handbook of Adult and Continuing Education.* San Francisco: Jossey-Bass, 2000.

Winant, H. *Racial Conditions: Politics, Theory, Comparisons.* Minneapolis: University of Minnesota Press, 1994.

JUANITA JOHNSON-BAILEY is an associate professor of adult education and women's studies at the University of Georgia, Athens.

5

This chapter expands the concept of diversity of learners to include many special needs and differences and examines effective strategies and technologies that open up options for all learners.

Teaching All Learners As If They Are Special

Nancy F. Gadbow

Respect for the uniqueness of each learner, learner-centered approaches, and building a relationship between the teacher-facilitator and the learner are concepts that have been presented for many years in adult education literature (Knowles, 1980; Brookfield, 1990; Smith, 1982). Indeed, these ideas underlie much of the writing in this book in regard to teaching adult learners. However, there are still areas of growth for everyone who works with adults in any of many different settings where learning happens. How many times I have been surprised by an adult learner! I had, unconsciously perhaps, made assumptions about an individual: what the needs are, what strategies would work, and, especially, what he or she thinks and believes about needs, abilities, goals, approaches, and learning strategies. As Vella (1994) aptly states, the learner becomes the teacher. This chapter explores ways in which teachers can become learners, especially co-learners, with adults who seek to learn in many diverse settings. When the many aspects of diversity that the learner and the teacher bring to the experience are considered, the challenges becomes even greater, but the range of possibilities for new learning to occur also can grow dramatically.

Each of the following learners has special needs and circumstances that affect his or her learning:

Ellen has macular degeneration, which greatly affects her vision and makes reading very difficult. Special accommodations, including some use of books on tape and screen readers, help her to continue to learn.
Scott has recently lost his job and is struggling with both financial concerns

NEW DIRECTIONS FOR ADULT AND CONTINUING EDUCATION, no. 93, Spring 2002 © Wiley Periodicals, Inc.

and damaged self-esteem. A learning program that allows him the flexibility to extend his time to complete courses he is taking makes it possible for him to take some time out but still finish these studies, as well as rebuild his confidence and gain important knowledge and skills.

John was fifty years old when he learned that he has severe dyslexia, which has a great impact on his learning. His family and school experiences had convinced him that he was, in his own words, "lazy and stupid." After some struggles to convince vocational rehabilitation services that he does have this specific disability, he now has a scanner and screen reader that allow him to "read" by listening. This very intelligent man is now pursuing a college degree.

Mary has repetitive motion syndrome that affects the use of her hands. Through some human service agencies and a mentoring program for persons with disabilities, she learned how to use speech-recognition software to "write" papers.

Susan's father recently had a heart attack, and she is spending a great deal of time and energy helping her parents. A college program that permits her to take a leave of absence makes it possible for her to continue her studies without penalty after a specific interim period.

Anne recently had a kidney with a cancerous tumor removed, and her recovery is delaying work on her doctoral dissertation. A program that permits a period of time off will make it possible for her to continue and complete a doctorate successfully.

How do these adult learners with a range of special needs and circumstances fit into the growing concept of diversity? As the United States looks at preparation of the workforce in this new century, addressing individual learners' needs and differences becomes even more critical. Age, gender, ethnicity, language, culture, disabilities, socioeconomic factors, geography, education, and past experiences are all part of the mix that a teacher or facilitator of learning must consider. However, many of these aspects of diversity largely have been ignored (Gadbow and Du Bois, 1998).

Rapidly developing on-line and other distance-education approaches have challenged the assumptions on which these traditional models of education in the United States have been based. However, the design and use of these new technologies have not necessarily considered learner diversity and needs. Whether in a college classroom, a corporate training seminar, or an on-line educational program, diverse needs of individual learners can be considered and addressed (Rossman, 2000; Hiemstra and Sisco, 1990).

This chapter considers these individual needs and the effective strategies and accommodations that can make the difference between success and failure for many learners. It challenges traditional approaches and methodologies that can inhibit learner success and offers a new paradigm for successful learning. The underlying premise is that there are different ways to learn and different ways to demonstrate learning. This somewhat radical view proposes consideration of the many needs, and combinations of needs, of adult learners and providing a range of accommodations (wherever reasonable and possible to do so), regardless of documentation of disabilities or other special needs.

Working with adults to help them identify their specific individual learning styles and differences and other special learning needs is the first responsibility of adult educators. Then the responsive teacher, facilitator, or mentor seeks effective strategies to adapt to these individual learning needs. In addition, beyond the objective to teach specific content is the broader objective to build competent self-directed learners who have developed the self-confidence and skills to guide and direct their own learning. As Smith (1982) pointed out in his groundbreaking work, helping adults learn how to learn is the most important thing a teacher ever does.

Perhaps most important, considering all learners as special means seeing the possibilities, as well as the problems or particular needs. It means seeing first what can be for a learner, as well as a realistic assessment of special needs to be addressed. Joe, a blind student, may not be able to use his eyes, but he can be helped to discover the possibilities and consider himself a competent independent learner, with many opportunities to contribute to his community.

The Special Needs of Adult Learners

Maria is an older Hispanic female who immigrated to the United States as a young woman; she speaks little English. She lives in a rural area, has scant work experience and a limited income, has a physical disability, and is a wheelchair user. Maria exemplifies how many different aspects of diversity can be present in one individual. An educator or trainer who is interested in helping Maria, and countless others like her, must be open to discovering the complex and multiple factors that are part of who she is.

A number of diversity aspects have been noted as being represented among adult learners. For those with special needs, a significant number have disabilities. According to a special Harris poll in 1998, 54 million people in the United States have at least one disability (National Organization on Disability, 1998). Beziat (1990) offers insight into the living conditions of many with disabilities: "Seventy-five percent of America's citizens with disabilities want to work. Less than 10 percent do. They are the poorest of the poor, living on a variety of social support programs that keep them unemployed and out of sight. Each year the government spends an estimated 60 billion dollars on various programs for those with disabilities, but less than 1 percent of those funds are spent to break the cycle of poverty and dependency" (p. 21). Beziat's statement makes a powerful case for the involvement of adult educators in helping these individuals successfully participate in educational programs. Of the more than 30 million individuals with disabilities between the ages of eighteen and sixty-two, most have not completed postsecondary education programs or successfully obtained meaningful employment, even though most are considered intellectually capable of pursuing higher education.

These special learners have various visible and invisible disabilities, including orthopedic, health related, hearing, learning, sight, and speech (Henderson, 1995). Mental health and emotional disabilities also cover a number of conditions with a range of severity. In addition, many people have more than one disability. Martha has multiple sclerosis and a learning disability. The needs that a learner may have can be minor ones or significant ones that require major accommodations.

Learning disabilities are complex and vary in degree of severity, and there is not a commonly accepted definition of a chronic learning difficulty (Jordan, 1996). However, scholars generally agree that persons with learning disabilities have some difficulty learning because of the way they receive or process information (Ross-Gordon, 1989). They may have difficulties related to listening, speaking, reading, writing, reasoning, or mathematical abilities. Persons with learning disabilities generally have average or above-average intelligence (Jordan, 1996). I have encountered a number of adults who describe having learning difficulties but have never been tested. Several have noted that one of their children has been diagnosed with a learning disability and wonder if that was the problem they had in school.

Differences that learners may have include disability, ethnicity, culture, language, age, gender, experience, and geography, as well as a combination of these characteristics. What do adult learners with all these diverse characteristics need to help them be successful learners? Their needs are as different as they are. Primarily, they need to be respected and treated as unique individuals who can learn and develop skills and abilities as competent self-directed learners.

Different circumstances may present specific barriers for learners: lack of vision; lack of hearing; lack of mobility due to a physical condition; tiredness or weakness due to a disease or treatment, such as chemotherapy; or difficulty with language as a non-English speaker. Other barriers may be less easy to identify. John lacks self-confidence and the ability to advocate for himself. A wheelchair user with cerebral palsy, he has been protected and advocated for much of his life by family and human service providers. He needs to learn skills as a self-advocate. Just as education programs may help people develop their study, writing, or critical thinking skills, self-advocacy training programs can be offered to help level the playing field and provide strategies for problem solving. Self-advocacy and self-directed learning are closely related concepts that teachers and facilitators can support (Hiemstra, 1998).

Conflict with Traditional Teaching-Learning Models and Settings

Many teachers and trainers of adult education programs have focused more on content and presenting material in group formats than on individual learning needs and differences. The history of public education in America, as well as that of traditional higher education, has added to this emphasis on content and measurement of institutionally directed outcomes. The result has been an educational system, mirrored in other adult education and corporate training programs, that fails to meet the needs of a substantial number of learners.

Traditional models of formal education present constraints that do not meet the needs of many learners, children as well as adults. The schedule and time of formal programs, location, transportation issues, large group format and instructional techniques, standardized tests, and rigid approaches to measurement of learning, as well as limited use of learning and assistive technologies, all present significant problems for many learners, including those with a range of disabilities (Gadbow and Du Bois, 1998). Perhaps even more limiting are the long-held attitudes that support the belief that there is one way to learn and one way to demonstrate learning. State education departments and regional accrediting bodies have reinforced these beliefs and solidified them into rigid guidelines. Many colleges and universities must still use the concept of "required seat time" as the norm. If it is violated, the college is in danger of losing its accreditation and funding.

Susan, who had to take time off to have major surgery, missed a number of sessions in her Introduction to Psychology course. After a period of recovery, she returned to this class, took the final exam, and earned an A grade. However, because she had missed a number of classes, she still failed the course. She was not permitted to show that she had learned the key concepts in this course and could demonstrate her learning sufficiently to earn credit.

The popularity of distance-learning programs is forcing higher education institutions to reconsider how they think about a course or program. As with traditional programs, the quality of a course or educational program is not necessarily determined by a set of specific guidelines, such as time, format, or structure.

Another persistent belief is that flexibility and alternative means of learning and demonstrating learning will water down the curriculum and lower standards. However, there is no evidence that learners with a range of special needs want to have standards lowered (Gadbow and Du Bois, 1998). To the contrary, persons with disabilities want to meet the requirements of educational and professional programs and be given equal consideration but not be treated differently or specially. Being able to demonstrate learning in alternative ways does not mean having less knowledge or skill. The end result must be that the individual is competent and is able to demonstrate the learning and meet all of the requirements of a particular degree or professional program.

Section 504 of the Rehabilitation Act of 1973 and the Americans with Disabilities Act of 1990 grew out of the disabilities rights movement that led to an increased social consciousness (Shapiro, 1993). These laws prohibit educational institutions from discriminating against individuals based on disability. In order to obtain learning accommodations, the individual must document a specific disability. The documentation that is required varies greatly and, as in the case of learning disabilities, may be a complex and costly process (Gadbow and Du Bois, 1998). What would happen if accommodations were given to any learner who requested them? The fear that has been expressed is that such an open policy would bog down higher education institutions with diverse requests for accommodations. However, if a more flexible structure and a range of options were present for courses and other educational programs, including distance learning, it is quite possible that the accommodations needed would be reasonable and manageable.

The corresponding probability is that the number of adult students who successfully complete college and other programs would increase dramatically. Dropouts and stopouts might be drastically cut. The high cost of recruiting and then losing students regularly might be reduced significantly. Furthermore, if these programs also prepared these adults with special needs with better resources and abilities as self-directed, competent learners, their preparation for entrance and success in the workplace may be greatly enhanced. The result could have substantial positive economic impact on society. Creative use of ideas in such a paradigm shift could combine a range of best strategies with cost-effective measures that allow for a variety and range of options without drastically increasing cost.

Applications of Effective Instructional Strategies and Approaches

If the constraints that have limited traditional higher education are suspended, it is possible to match creatively appropriate methods and techniques with specific needs of individual learners, whether in a classroom, an on-line setting, or an independent learning situation.

I have the advantage of teaching at a college where guided independent study is the primary mode of learning. In these one-on-one sessions, faculty mentors have the opportunity to discover more about these adult learners and their needs, learning styles, and interests. Their learning activities and strategies, as well as some content areas, can be tailored to the individual. In her discussion of mentoring, Zachary (2000) emphasizes the importance of building such a relationship with each learner.

How can teacher-facilitators learn about adult students and their specific needs in traditional classroom or training situations or in distance-learning programs? How can these students be treated in special ways?

Opportunities to interact with learners individually or in small groups can be built into all types of learning experiences, including classroom and on-line programs. Various assessment tools, including learning style inventories, also can be used to help the learner and facilitator understand the best strategies to use to meet specific needs.

Attitudes and responses of teacher-facilitators and other education and service providers to adults with a range of needs and situations can greatly affect the opportunity for them to succeed in learning programs. Sometimes learning accommodations are needed, including a range of technologies. At other times, patience, understanding, and acceptance are needed. Frequently, providing a climate that fosters self-development and self-advocacy is important for adults with special needs to discover how they learn best and what strategies and accommodations they need to be successful learners. Flexibility in programs, schedules, and use of alternative means to demonstrate knowledge and skills are essential.

Teacher-facilitators who understand learning styles and differences and seek to individualize learning, even in a classroom setting, generally use a range of approaches. Brookfield (1990) describes "teaching responsively": "I must be willing to find out about students' backgrounds, cultures, outlooks, and expectations and, on the basis of this knowledge, find ways of communicating the importance of thinking critically that relate directly to these" (p. 23). He also encourages teachers to adapt their content and approaches to match the ways students are learning.

Students also can be actively involved in experimenting with approaches used in a classroom. If they are asked to be part of an experiment, they often take some ownership and provide useful feedback to enhance and improve a method being used. Some of the work that has been done on collaborative and group learning has shown that successful teachers and trainers set up the approach carefully and gradually involve the class in group activities that have been established with great care and detail (Bosworth, 1994; Cramer, 1994).

Rossman (2000) applies andragogical principles and gives examples of how options can be expanded and developed to meet individual and alternative needs of learners in distance-learning programs. In teaching Web-based courses, I have found it important to vary the structure and format to meet the special needs of the learners. Blending teaching approaches and technologies can help match different learning styles. For example, one instructor mails a video to each distance learner to complement the primarily Web-based course. The reflective adult educator learns from each teaching experience and refreshes and builds strategies that are uniquely designed for the individual learner or specific group of learners.

Alma came to the Untied States to earn a master's degree in adult education at a major university. Her country in Africa, where she coordinated an educational program for women, was supporting her. Her past educational experiences had been very formal and traditional; she "sat for exams" at midterm and the end of courses. When the first course in the adult education graduate program presented her with flexible options, choices, and the use of learning contracts (Knowles, 1980), she was unsure how to begin. Fortunately for Alma, Roger Hiemstra, a well-known adult educator who has contributed many publications to the field, was the professor of that first class. He provided her with support, mentoring, and guidance as she developed her first learning contract.

As a doctoral student in that same course (also my first in the program), I made the assumption that contract learning and other aspects of self-directed learning would not work well for Alma. My assumptions were wrong. Some months later, I found myself in another course with Alma, also taught by Hiemstra. He began with an explanation of how contract learning would be used. She interrupted him to give an enthusiastic testimony regarding contract learning. She had learned how to use it effectively and now resented traditional courses she had taken in other departments of the university with a midterm and final exam and few, if any, options for learners.

With the guidance and mentoring of Hiemstra and other adult education faculty, Alma had matured and developed new skills to become a competent self-directed learner. How often do we make assumptions about learners who come with many different needs, backgrounds, cultures, and experiences, and how often do we fail to offer individualized approaches to help them learn how to learn?

Technologies with New Options for Learners with Special Needs

Scherer (1996) describes many of the ways that technology is affecting the lives of persons with disabilities. Assistive technologies are opening the world of learning and the world of work for many who had not previously been considered candidates for either realm. Independence, as well as the ability to earn money and contribute in meaningful jobs, can be traced for many to these new technologies. The goal is to match the appropriate technologies to meet the unique needs of each individual (Scherer and Galvin, 1996).

The Internet is developing opportunities for people with disabilities to obtain information that is accessible. "When web pages are designed with a concern for accessibility from the beginning, they can be read through the use of technology by virtually all people with disabilities" (Du Bois, 1998, p. 9). Voice-recognition and voice-activated computers allow persons with various disabilities, such as visual impairments, learning disabilities, and some mobility issues, to be able to access information and "write papers."

However, I have found that many students, or potential students, do not know what they do not know. Totally unfamiliar with such technology, unless connected with rehabilitation services, technology providers, or mentors who have used the specific technology for their particular disabilities, they will not obtain the appropriate technology and the necessary training to use it effectively. These connections can make the difference between success and failure in an educational program. The teacher or other learning support office in an educational institution can connect the learner with the appropriate service providers. The teacher need not become an expert in all types of special needs and all types of technologies. However, knowing a few key resources both regionally and nationally can be a major step

Table 5.1. Disability-Related Organizations

Organization	Purpose	Web Address
Association on Higher Education and Disability (AHEAD)	International organization committed to full participation in higher education for persons with disabilities	www.ahead.org
National Institute on Disabilities and Rehabilitation Research (NIDRR)	Sponsors of the Office of Special Education and Rehabilitative Service; conducts research and activities to maximize inclusion of persons with disabilities	www.ed.gov/offices /OSERS/NIDRR
National Organization on Disability (NOD)	Promotes participation of persons with disabilities in all aspects of society	www.nod.org
Office of Special Education and Rehabilitative Service, Rehabilitation Services Administration (OSERS/ RSA)	Carries out titles of Rehabilitation Act of 1973: services, training, research	www.ed.gov/offices /OSERS/RSA
Rehabilitation Engineering and Assistive Technology Society of North America (RESNA)	Interdisciplinary association of people with a common interest in technology and disability	www.resna.org
World Institute on Disability (WID)	Nonprofit international public policy center; research on disability issues	www.wid.org

in helping a learner. The regional vocational rehabilitation agency and Independent Living Center are two sources that can be helpful in connecting a learner with special needs to appropriate services. Table 5.1 lists some of the national and international organizations that deal with disability issues.

Conclusion

Although this chapter has focused primarily on adult learners with special needs, the concepts apply to any other situation where adults are learning. All adult learners have a combination of unique characteristics and needs that call for assessment and design of unique accommodations and strategies to help each person learn effectively, whether in classrooms or individually and in a range of alternative learning settings and circumstances. Everything learned from working with individual learners with special needs can be applied to adult learners in general. To teach all learners as if they are special is indeed the mark of the true adult educator.

References

Beziat, C. "Educating America's Last Minority: Adult Education's Role in the Americans with Disabilities Act." *Adult Learning,* 1990, *2,* 21–23.

Bosworth, K. "Developing Collaborative Skills in College Students." In K. Bosworth and S. J. Hamilton (eds.), *Collaborative Learning: Underlying Processes and Effective Techniques.* New Directions for Teaching and Learning, no. 59. San Francisco: Jossey-Bass, 1994.

Brookfield, S. D. *The Skillful Teacher.* San Francisco: Jossey-Bass, 1990.

Cramer, S. F. "Assessing Effectiveness in the Collaborative Classroom." In K. Bosworth and S. J. Hamilton (eds.), *Collaborative Learning: Underlying Processes and Effective Techniques.* New Directions for Teaching and Learning, no. 59. San Francisco: Jossey-Bass, 1994.

Du Bois, D. A. "Adult Learners with Disabilities: A New Imperative for Adult Educators." *New Horizons in Adult Education,* 1998, *2.* [www.nova.edu/~aed/newhorizons .html.]

Gadbow, N. F., and Du Bois, D. A. *Adult Learners with Special Needs: Strategies and Resources for Postsecondary Education and Workplace Training.* Malabar, Fla.: Krieger, 1998.

Henderson, C. *College Freshmen with Disabilities: A Triennial Statistical Profile.* Washington, D.C.: American Council on Education, HEATH Resource Center, 1995.

Hiemstra, R. "Self-Advocacy and Self-Directed Learning: A Potential Confluence for Enhanced Personal Empowerment." Paper presented at the SUNY Empire State College Conference: Disabled, But Enabled and Empowered, Rochester, N.Y., Mar. 20, 1998. [www-distance.syr.edu/advocacy.html.]

Hiemstra, R., and Sisco, B. *Individualizing Instruction: Making Learning Personal, Empowering, and Successful.* San Francisco: Jossey-Bass, 1990.

Jordan, D. R. *Teaching Adults with Learning Disabilities.* Malabar, Fla.: Krieger, 1996.

Knowles, M. S. *The Modern Practice of Adult Education: From Pedagogy to Andragogy.* (Rev. and updated ed.) River Grove, Ill.: Follett, 1980.

National Organization on Disability/Louis Harris and Associates. *Survey Program on Participation and Attitudes.* Washington, D.C.: National Organization on Disability/ Louis Harris and Associates, July 23, 1998.

Ross-Gordon, J. M. *Adults with Learning Disabilities: An Overview for the Adult Educator.* Columbus, Ohio: ERIC Clearinghouse on Adult, Career, and Vocational Education, Center on Education and Training for Employment, Ohio State University, 1989. (ED 315 664)

Rossman, M. H. "Andragogy and Distance Education: Together in the New Millennium." *New Horizons in Adult Education,* 2000, *14.* [nova.edu/~aed/newhorizons.html.]

Scherer, M. J. *Living in the State of Stuck: How Technology Impacts the Lives of People with Disabilities.* Cambridge, Mass.: Brookline Books, 1996.

Scherer, M. J., and Galvin, J. C. *Evaluating, Selecting, and Using Appropriate Assistive Technology.* Gaithersburg, Md.: Aspen, 1996.

Shapiro, J. *No Pity: People with Disabilities Forging a New Civil Rights Movement.* New York: Time Books, 1993.

Smith, R. M. *Learning How to Learn: Applied Theory for Adults.* Cambridge: Cambridge University Press, 1982.

Vella, J. *Learning to Listen, Learning to Teach.* San Francisco: Jossey-Bass, 1994.
Zachary, L. J. *The Mentor's Guide: Facilitating Effective Learning Relationships.* San Francisco: Jossey-Bass, 2000.

NANCY F. GADBOW is mentor/coordinator at Empire State College, State University of New York, Canandaigua.

6

In teaching for transformation, teachers set the stage and provide the environment in which students can articulate and critically reflect on their assumptions and perspectives.

Teaching for Transformation

Patricia Cranton

Andrew was a student in Methods and Strategies in Adult Education, a course offered within the New Brunswick Community College Instructor Development Program, which is mandatory for all new college instructors. One goal of the program is to prepare individuals who are hired on the basis of their experience and expertise in their profession or trade for the world of teaching. The summer courses are intensive: students are in class five hours a day, five days a week, and many choose to live in residence. Andrew was proud to come from a military background and equally proud that he was going to be teaching in a highly technical field.

Andrew's thinking and way of expressing himself was clear, organized, and practical, and he viewed things in absolute terms. From the course, he wanted specific rules to follow to guarantee successful teaching. He expected that I would be able to teach him exactly what he needed to do as a teacher. When this turned out not to be the case, Andrew was frustrated, even angry, with me and the entire program, which he viewed as useless. Our textbook, *No One Way: Teaching and Learning in Higher Education* (Cranton, 1998), did not help matters. Day after painful day, Andrew struggled to find the answers he was seeking amid our discussions of self-directed learning, teaching styles, and individual differences. Andrew was intellectually curious; he devoured the readings not only in search of the right answer but also because it was his nature to want to understand.

Sometime during the second week, after about forty hours of class time, there came a moment of profound silence when we all focused our attention on Andrew. I am not sure how he signaled to us that he had something important to say, but we all knew it. Breaking out of his confusion and resentment, Andrew announced that he saw, accepted, and clearly understood the shades of gray existing in knowledge about teaching. He understood that knowledge about teaching is communicative in nature and socially constructed. He saw that knowing how to teach his subject area was different from knowing his subject area. The moment was joyful and transformative.

We all hope for such moments in our work with students. But how do we teach for transformation? As Andrew discovered, there is no one way, and as Pratt explores in Chapter One of this volume, one size does not fit all. In this chapter, I provide an overview of transformative learning theory and explore ways in which we might set up conditions to foster transformation.

Kinds of Knowledge

Although Mezirow (1991) sees transformative learning as a primary goal of all adult education, and most of us would agree, it is not the only goal. The larger framework within which transformative learning theory fits is based on Habermas's (1971) three kinds of knowledge: instrumental, communicative (which Habermas calls practical), and emancipatory.

Instrumental knowledge is cause-and-effect, objective knowledge derived from scientific methodologies. The acquisition of instrumental knowledge is a goal of education in the trades, technologies, and sciences. This is the kind of knowledge Andrew was seeking, but not finding, in my course.

Communicative knowledge is the understanding of ourselves, others, and the social norms of the community or society in which we live. It is derived through language and validated by consensus among people. The acquisition of communicative knowledge is a goal in the study of human relations, political and social systems, and education.

Emancipatory knowledge, the self-awareness that frees us from constraints, is a product of critical reflection and critical self-reflection. Gaining emancipatory knowledge can be a goal in all facets of adult education, as we critically question, for example, the role of technology, which is in itself instrumental knowledge, or the underlying assumptions of a political system, which is in itself communicative knowledge. It is an explicit goal in life skills learning, literacy programs, self-help groups, women's studies courses, and community action groups. The acquisition of emancipatory knowledge is transformative.

Transformative Learning Theory

At its core, transformative learning theory is elegantly simple. Through some event, which could be as traumatic as losing a job or as ordinary as an unexpected question, an individual becomes aware of holding a limiting or distorted view. If the individual critically examines this view, opens herself to alternatives, and consequently changes the way she sees things, she has transformed some part of how she makes meaning out of the world.

Mezirow (1991, 1997, 2000) developed the theory of transformative learning through a careful integration of theories, models, and ideas from a wide variety of sources. The theory continues to evolve through the inclusion of new perspectives on adult learning and development.

We expect what has happened in the past to happen again. If we failed to understand mathematics, we expect to continue to fail in this subject. If our boss has always been critical of our work, we expect her to continue to be critical. If our parents told us we were stupid, we think we are. The habits of mind that are established may have to do with our sense of self, interpretation of social systems and issues, morals and religious beliefs, and job-related knowledge.

It is easier and safer to maintain habits of mind than to change. It may take a significant or dramatic event to lead us to question assumptions and beliefs. Other times, though, it is an incremental process in which we gradually change bits of how we see things, not even realizing a transformation has taken place until afterward.

Critical reflection is the means by which we work through beliefs and assumptions, assessing their validity in the light of new experiences or knowledge, considering their sources, and examining underlying premises. It helps to talk to others, exchanging opinions and ideas, receiving support and encouragement, and engaging in discourse where alternatives are seriously weighed and evidence brought forth. Insight, intuition, emotion, relationships, and personality may also play roles. Dirkx (1997) argues that purely rational explanations of transformation are inadequate. Carter (2000) finds little evidence of rational discourse in her research, though relationships among people are pivotal. I propose there may be differences based on psychological type preferences in the ways in which people revise their perspectives (Cranton, 1994, 1996).

Facets of Transformative Learning

If we are to understand how to teach for transformation, we need to recognize the various facets of the process. Transformative learning is not a linear process, yet there is some progression to it, perhaps spiral-like (Cranton, 2000). We cannot critically reflect on an assumption until we are aware of it. We cannot engage in discourse on something we have not identified. We cannot change a habit of mind without thinking about it in some way.

In his earlier work, Mezirow (1975) names steps or stages leading to transformation, starting with a disorienting dilemma and ending with restored equilibrium. In most of the writing on transformative learning, many of these facets of the process remain in some form, though they are no longer seen as steps. Here, I identify seven such facets as a rough guide to helping us set up a learning environment to promote transformation:

- An activating event that typically exposes a discrepancy between what a person has always assumed to be true and what has just been experienced, heard, or read
- Articulating assumptions, that is, recognizing underlying assumptions that have been uncritically assimilated and are largely unconscious
- Critical self-reflection, that is, questioning and examining assumptions in terms of where they came from, the consequences of holding them, and why they are important
- Being open to alternative viewpoints
- Engaging in discourse, where evidence is weighed, arguments assessed, alternative perspectives explored, and knowledge constructed by consensus
- Revising assumptions and perspectives to make them more open and better justified
- Acting on revisions, behaving, talking, and thinking in a way that is congruent with transformed assumptions or perspectives

Teaching Strategies

There are no particular teaching methods that guarantee transformative learning. A provocative statement in a lecture, a story told by a fellow student, or an argument set out in an article are just as likely to stimulate critical self-reflection as is the most carefully crafted exercise. Often, neither we as teachers nor the transforming student can pinpoint just what initiated or sustained the process. A lot of what happens is within the student, and the teacher just happens to say or do something that hooks into that person's thoughts or feelings. When Andrew and I tried to understand what promoted his transformed assumption about the nature of knowledge, the best we could come up with was that he felt personally challenged by ideas expressed in the classroom and in his reading.

I think it is this environment of challenge that underlies teaching for transformation. Although this challenge must be combined with safety, support, and a sense of learner empowerment, it is, at the center, a challenge of our beliefs, assumptions, and perspectives that leads us to question ourselves.

I propose strategies for each of the facets of transformative learning, but I do not intend to imply that we can make such clear distinctions in practice between either facets or strategies. In choosing a specific strategy and in knowing what is happening with our students, we may rely on intuition or perhaps a tacit understanding of the teaching and learning context.

Creating an Activating Event. In order to bring about a catalyst for transformation, we need to expose students to viewpoints that may be discrepant with their own. Films, documentaries, novels, short stories, and poems often portray unusual perspectives in dramatic and interesting ways. I am surprised by how often the students I work with choose to express a transformative experience in a song, drawing, or sculpture. I suspect that if I were more knowledgeable about these art forms, I could also use them as a catalyst for learning.

Whenever possible, we should use readings to present ideas from more than one point of view. We need to encourage students to seek out controversial or unusual ways of understanding a topic. And in our own presentation of ideas, we should always ask, "What if we looked at this from another perspective?" or "What assumptions underlie this viewpoint?"

Articulating Assumptions. Articulating assumptions is hard. It may seem impossible to answer the question, "What assumption are you making here?" Our assumptions are deeply embedded in our childhood, community, and culture. Brookfield's (1990) technique of critical questioning can be helpful. Questions are crafted so as to encourage students to describe what they believe and how they came to believe it. For example, I might ask, "Do you believe intelligence declines with age?" followed by, "How would you describe intelligence?" and "Is your view based on your own experience or the experience of someone you know?" or "What have you read or heard that supports that view?"

Student autobiographies can be a powerful technique for unearthing assumptions. Autobiographies can be specific to one aspect of a person's life: "Tell the story of how you became a teacher and developed as a teacher [or any other profession]." Or they may be personal. The use of autobiographies is enhanced when the educator provides supportive comments and asks questions such as, "How did this come about?" "How did you make this decision?" "What are you assuming here?"

A colleague of mine designed a form of autobiography that he calls a time capsule (Laurence Cohen, e-mail to the author, 2000). Students are asked to come up with a collection of objects representing important aspects of their life and put the objects into a box or container (the time capsule). Students act as archeologists in pairs or small groups to analyze and understand the importance of each object in the time capsule. The question, "Why is this object important?" is also addressing, "What assumption do you make in including this object as representative of your life?"

I have found metaphor analysis (Deshler, 1990) to be useful in encouraging the articulation of assumptions. Students generate metaphors relevant to a topic under discussion. For example, they might list metaphors for summer school as including a prison, a zoo, a cave, and a kaleidoscope. The metaphors are then unpacked by asking, "What are the characteristics of a prison that are also characteristics of summer school?" Students may say, "We have to be here, it's a punishment, and we can only look out the window." Each of these responses can then be discussed in relation to underlying assumptions: "Why is summer school seen as a punishment?" "What are we assuming about summer school?"

Critical Self-Reflection. To encourage critical self-reflection, we need to provide the opportunity for students to question their assumptions: to examine what they think and how they feel and consider the consequences of holding certain assumptions. Critical self-reflection may take place in the classroom, but it is perhaps more likely to take place outside it. What we do in the classroom is set the stage for what may take place when our students are driving home, cooking supper, going for a walk, or telling someone about their day.

Critical incidents, originally developed as a research technique, have been popularized by Brookfield (1995) as a means of fostering critical self-reflection. Students are asked to recall a best or worst experience, usually within a specific context, such as their worst teaching experience or their best interaction with a supervisor. They describe the incident in terms of what happened, who was involved, what made it a best or worst experience, and how it could have turned out differently. Analysis of the incidents, done in either small groups or the whole class, helps people examine their assumptions and provides a structure for reflection on practice.

Reflective journals are widely used in adult education and for some, but not all, students are a good vehicle for critical self-reflection. Students who are more introverted than extroverted find journals especially helpful. Although the literature contains many suggestions for how to structure a journal, I find it best to leave the format open so that students can write as they please. I suggest that they not only report on what happened but also include their thoughts, reactions, and feelings and pay special attention to writing about why they think or feel as they do. I offer to read their journals if they would like me to, which gives the uncertain student a chance to validate his journal with me. When students give me the opportunity to read their work, I encourage further critical self-reflection through comments as questions.

Modeling critical self-reflection and setting up an environment in which critical self-reflection is a group norm may be one of the most important ways to teach for transformation. We should make a point of openly questioning our own perspectives and support students' efforts to do the same. Although it may seem uncomfortable at first, especially if we are used to being the voice of authority in the classroom, a questioning atmosphere can quickly become quite natural.

Openness to Alternatives. Being open to perspectives different from our own can be exceedingly difficult. Students may articulate their assumptions and reflect on them but shut down when faced with accepting alternatives. What we have to try to do in our teaching is to create safe and enjoyable ways for people to try on different points of view—ways of acting out or talking about alternatives.

Role plays are especially useful in giving students a chance to try on an alternative perspective without giving up their own. Role plays can be used in many contexts, and they may be informal and spontaneous or scripted and formal. In order to nurture openness to alternatives, students should take on roles that are opposed to their own perspective. For example, in a course on research methods, I asked students to work in groups of three where one person adhered to the empirical-analytical paradigm, the second to the interpretive paradigm, and the third to the critical paradigm. In the role play, they were to discuss how to approach a particular research problem. Students' roles were assigned so as to go against their preference for one paradigm over another.

Critical debates (Brookfield, 1990) serve a similar purpose but without the use of roles. A controversial issue is selected, one for which students in the group hold contrasting views. Students identify their view and debate the issue taking the stance that is opposite their own. This may seem hard at first, and students often say they cannot think of any arguments, but once the debate is underway, it can be a source of quite astounding insights. Students also seem to find the process to be quite amusing; it is easy to laugh at yourself when you are saying the opposite of what you think when the exercise is treated like a game. Meanwhile, you are opening yourself to the possibility of thinking in a new way.

Another similar simple strategy is to ask students to write letters or memos from a different perspective. For example, managers engaged in a leadership workshop could be asked to write letters from their staff to themselves outlining the changes in the workplace they would like to see. Or students could write letters representing theoretical viewpoints, especially those viewpoints with which they do not agree—a letter from Freud to a female patient, for instance.

Discourse. Engaging in discourse, as opposed to regular discussion, can seem stilted or artificial. I have tried to do this by first presenting and discussing the optimal conditions for discourse: having accurate and complete information, being free from coercion and distorting self-deception, weighing evidence and assessing arguments, being open to alternative perspectives, critically reflecting on presuppositions, having equal opportunity to participate, and accepting informed consensus as valid knowledge (Mezirow, 1991). To some extent, this works. It also helps to ask one or two students to be observers, noting when participants, for example, resort to persuasion rather than evidence.

Addressing the same issue in two ways—through ordinary discussion and then through discourse—helps students see the difference in the two ways of communicating. I have also videotaped discourse, giving students the opportunity to see when and how they demonstrate the optimal conditions.

Dialogue journals provide another format for discourse. Students work in pairs or even triads. They may have one journal that they pass from person to person, responding to each other's ideas, or they may all write simultaneously, exchanging journal entries and commenting on each other's writing (this yields, in the end, two or three journals rather than one). If students remain conscious of the conditions of discourse, it sometimes seems easier to work toward them in writing than in conversation.

Revision of Assumptions and Perspectives. Teaching for transformation is setting the stage and providing the opportunity. When students actually revise their assumptions or larger frames of reference, there is little we can do aside from giving support. The process may be painful for some, and we need to acknowledge this, or it may be joyous for others, and we can celebrate with the student. Whenever possible, we should make the time for one-on-one interaction with a student who is changing beliefs.

Perhaps even more important, we can encourage students to connect with each other—either fellow students within the same class or students who have taken the same course or program on other occasions. A class listserv or the simple exchange of e-mail addresses and telephone numbers can be an important resource. Formal learning networks or support groups can be established, but generally this kind of support works best when students initiate it in their own way. Depending on the context, we can also suggest that students link up with discussion groups, professional associations, or other resources where people will have had experiences similar to theirs.

Acting on Revisions.   To help students act on their revised assumptions or perspectives, we need to set up situations where they have the opportunity to do so. Quite often, such action falls outside the time and place where we work with students, but there may still be some things we can do. Experiential learning projects, where students go out into the real world—schools, hospitals, businesses—can give them a chance to try out their transformed views. Experiential learning may be built into a program, but if it is not, we can arrange field trips or site visits to serve the same purpose. Students can be asked to keep a log or journal of the experience, especially noting how they felt and how others reacted to their views.

If experiential learning projects are not feasible, it is sometimes possible to set up a simulation of a real setting where students have the opportunity to practice or talk about their new learning. Simulated committee meetings or fund drives, mock parliaments, and microteaching are examples of such activities.

Finally, we can help students set up action plans for when they leave the course or workshop. This can be as simple as asking participants to write down two or three concrete things they will do, or it can be a more formal plan with goals, strategies for achieving those goals, and mechanisms for getting feedback from others. The more we pay attention to how students will act on their revised assumptions and perspectives, the more we can ease that process for them. Even ordinary conversations about what people will do when they, for example, return to the workplace from a retreat will help. In some contexts, it may be possible to plan a follow-up meeting for participants to discuss how they have acted on their transformation.

Conclusion

When a student transforms her assumptions, becoming open to alternatives and new ways of thinking, it is a magical moment in teaching. We cannot teach transformation. We often cannot even identify how or why it happens.

But we can teach as though the possibility always exists that a student will have a transformative experience.

There are no special methods that guarantee transformation, although transformation is always one of our goals. In every strategy we use, we need to provide an ever-changing balance of challenge, support, and learner empowerment. Sometimes to ask the right challenging question at the right moment is the most important thing we can do. At other times, it is essential to validate a student's thoughts or feelings. And at yet another time, we need to say, "This is up to you now," because in the end, it is the student who chooses to transform.

References

Brookfield, S. D. *The Skillful Teacher*. San Francisco: Jossey-Bass, 1990.

Brookfield, S. D. *Becoming a Critically Reflective Teacher*. San Francisco: Jossey-Bass, 1995.

Carter, T. "Learning in Relationships: A Heuristic Study of Midcareer Women's Experiences in Transformative Learning Through Developmental Relationships." Unpublished doctoral dissertation, George Washington University, 2000.

Cranton, P. *Understanding and Promoting Transformative Learning*. San Francisco: Jossey-Bass, 1994.

Cranton, P. *Professional Development as Transformative Learning*. San Francisco: Jossey-Bass, 1996.

Cranton, P. *No One Way: Teaching and Learning in Higher Education*. Toronto: Wall & Emerson, 1998.

Cranton, P. "Individuation and Authenticity in Transformative Learning." Paper presented at the Third International Conference on Transformative Learning, New York, N.Y., Oct. 2000.

Deshler, D., "Metaphor Analysis: Exorcising Social Ghosts." In J. Mezirow and others (eds.), *Fostering Critical Reflection in Adulthood*. San Francisco: Jossey-Bass, 1990.

Dirkx, J. "Nurturing the Soul in Adult Learning." In P. Cranton (ed.), *Transformative Learning in Action: Insights from Practice*. New Directions in Adult and Continuing Education, no. 74. San Francisco: Jossey-Bass, 1997.

Habermas, J. *Knowledge and Human Interests*. Boston: Beacon Press, 1971.

Mezirow, J. *Education for Perspective Transformation: Women's Reentry Programs in Community Colleges*. New York: Center for Adult Education, Teachers College, Columbia University, 1975.

Mezirow, J. *Transformative Dimensions of Adult Learning*. San Francisco: Jossey-Bass, 1991.

Mezirow, J. "Transformative Learning: Theory to Practice." In P. Cranton (ed.), *Transformative Learning in Action: Insights from Practice*. New Directions in Adult and Continuing Education, no. 74. San Francisco: Jossey-Bass, 1997.

Mezirow, J., and others. *Learning as Transformation: Critical Perspectives on a Theory in Progress*. San Francisco: Jossey-Bass, 2000.

PATRICIA CRANTON *is professor of adult education at the University of New Brunswick in Fredericton, Canada.*

7

This chapter focuses on teaching as dialogue and the potential that such an approach offers to bringing about quantum learning.

Quantum Learning: Teaching as Dialogue

Jane Vella

I recently enjoyed a day at the Rodin exhibit at the North Carolina Museum of Art. I was deeply touched by Rodin's own words on a note by his famous sculpture, *The Thinker*. "Notice," said the sculptor, "how the thinker is clearly thinking with his toes." The energy shown in the rippling muscles in the legs of Rodin's thinker is measured by quanta. A quantum, in the language of physics, is a measure of energy.

The energy manifest in the engagement of adult learners around a relevant, immediate learning task is a sign of quantum learning. The critical and creative response of adult learners to a respectful, significant open question is a sign of quantum learning. The dialogue in small groups that moves content beyond itself into the context and lives of the group is a sign of quantum learning.

Quantum Learning Defined

Quantum learning is that which uses all of the neural networks in the brain, putting things together in idiosyncratic and personal ways to make significant meaning. Zohar (1997) describes quantum thinking in terms of three functions of the brain: the one-to-one leap of energy between neurons on a neural tract, which she calls serial thinking; the leap of energy in a pattern across a neural network, which she calls patterned or associative thinking; and the explosion of energy throughout the whole brain using a network of neural networks, which she names quantum thinking. Here are some examples:

NEW DIRECTIONS FOR ADULT AND CONTINUING EDUCATION, no. 93, Spring 2002 © Wiley Periodicals, Inc.

Serial thinking: What is the capital of Portugal? The capital of Portugal is Lisbon.

Patterned thinking: What do you notice about many of the capital cities of Europe? Many of the capitals of Europe are on waterways.

Quantum thinking: Political and economic realities are and have always been deeply entwined. How is the Internet a global waterway? Where is the capital?

Teaching as dialogue invites quantum thinking and quantum learning; it invites adult learners to "think with their toes." I suggest the quality of such learning is one answer to current problems in education at every level.

The Dialogue Approach to Quantum Learning

The dialogue approach to teaching, using learning tasks and principles and practices set out in Vella (1996), was designed at the JUBILEE Popular Education Center in Raleigh, North Carolina, to enhance the teaching practice of adult educators in every field: community development, health, agriculture, literacy, higher education, and business. JUBILEE Fellows have completed a rigorous five-day introductory course entitled Learning to Listen, Learning to Teach.

In that course, learners use learning tasks to examine the roots of their own epistemology and practice, work with classic concepts of sound learning from sages like John Dewey, Kurt Lewin, Malcolm Knowles, and Paulo Freire, and then design and use this new teaching approach in two separate events. All of the work in this five-day course is done in dialogue, in both small groups and the larger group of ten to twelve participants.

There are now over three thousand JUBILEE Fellows around the world who use the dialogue approach in their work and celebrate the results with their adult students. Some of them have gone on to do an advanced design course and a master teacher course and a parallel course on evaluation. As I designed these courses and wrote the books describing this practical dialogue approach to teaching, I did not know that we were in fact moving toward quantum learning. The "enhancement" effected by this dialogue approach to teaching can now be understood in the light of recent research in physics. Zohar (1997) holds that dialogue is the tool for creating quantum thinking.

Principles and Practices: Toward the Dialogue Approach

Among the fifty principles and practices to ensure the dialogue approach to teaching (described in detail in Vella, 1996) are these:

dialogue
respect

immediacy
relevance
engagement
sequence
use of physical, affective, and cognitive means to learning
time
titles
learning tasks
open questions
lavish affirmation
case studies
stories
warm-ups
feedback
closure
consultative and deliberative voices
small groups
visuals and charts
the use of video clips
charts
music, art, and poetry
learners as subjects of their own learning
The Seven Steps of Planning (WHO, WHY, WHEN, WHERE, WHAT, WHAT FOR, HOW)
inclusion
inductive and deductive approaches
praxis
safety
humor
autonomy
congruence
documentation

At one point in the Learning to Listen, Learning to Teach course, fifty cards with these principles and practices are spread across a table. The group is invited to select one that they could omit, that is, one they think is not necessary to the JUBILEE Dialogue approach. They cannot.

Here is the paradox: the dialogue approach is highly structured to invite spontaneity. Campbell (1988) describes the Buddha's ineffable experience under the Bo Tree. After contemplating the gift of his illumination for days in absolute stillness, the Buddha said: "This cannot be taught." That, to me, means that the physical, emotional, and cognitive experience of learning is always a personal, idiosyncratic one. One must think with one's own toes. The design of effective teaching through dialogue keeps that paradox in mind.

The axioms laid out in Vella (1996) show some of the enigmatic aspects of this dialogue approach—for example:

Don't tell what you can ask; don't ask if you know the answer, tell, in dialogue. Pray for doubt.
Be careful about having too much What for your When.
What is needed for effective teaching is—in this order—time, time and time.
A learning task is a task for the learner! [p. 45]

A colleague from South Africa challenged me once after she read my book *Training Through Dialogue* (1996): "You have given the course away!" She was referring to the fact that the entire first course is described in that text. I smiled and replied, "If anyone can teach using this dialogue approach after having read that book, more power to her!"

We know that effective quantum learning involves more than reading and more than the sharing of information. As we teach these vital principles in the course, we use the principles and practices we are teaching. Learners are struck by the congruence and see how important it is to be and do what you are teaching.

Masters of Quantum Learning: Bohr, Bohm, Freire, Lewin, Oliver, Zohar

The conceptual framework behind this particular design of a dialogue approach is eclectic. However, there is a common strain in the selected sources: all speak to the need for a transformation of educational practice toward personal meaning making.

Neils Bohr and David Bohm. Bohr made the daring breakthrough in physics to quantum theories, and Bohm's work on dialogue (Bohm and Peat, 1987) has led to a serious consideration of this as a scientific and viable means of communication not only of information but also of knowledge and skills.

Paulo Freire. As a professor at the Institute of Education of the University of Dar es Salaam in 1964, I was close to burnout. My desire was to teach the Tanzanian teachers in the institute and university programs to be not only effective teachers but also autonomous and culturally appropriate teachers. Everything I did as a professor felt like, and indeed was, a part of the colonial whole. Although Tanzania was independent by this time, the colonial ethos persisted.

I was seriously thinking about a career change when a colleague gave me a copy of Paulo Freire's *Pedagogy of the Oppressed* ([1970] 1993). In many countries, the book was banned. Happily, in Julius Nyerere's nascent Tanzania, it was welcomed.

While I was reading it, I received a telephone call: Paulo Freire was in town and would be giving a lecture at the Institute of Adult Education that afternoon. I dropped everything and ran to the institute, somehow knowing this event was critical in my young life.

Freire warmly shared his delight at being in Africa and told about his work in Brazil and Chile in literacy programs that used the theories he shared in his seminal book. I remember the joy in the eyes of all the listeners, who, like me, were searching for an alternative to dominating teaching practices.

As we greeted Paulo at the end, I asked, "Do many women tell you they love you after these lectures?"

"Oh, yes," he replied.

"Many Catholic nuns?" I pursued.

"Yes. In fact, I am a member of a Catholic religious community of nuns: the Maryknoll Sisters! The sisters in Chile, after a course I taught them, made me a member."

We laughed together, and a lifelong love affair began.

Freire as a seminal thinker and philosopher, an epistemologist and political strategist, wrote and taught densely. Many of my students found the English translation of his writing hard to understand. I urged them to persevere because no second-hand version would serve them as well. His descriptions of dialogue and his analysis of the implications of the opposite of dialogue that he called "the banking approach" are the foundations of what we call the JUBILEE dialogue approach. Freire's work takes Bohr and Bohm's work to school.

Freire's political, epistemological, personal, strategic perspective is at the heart of JUBILEE. I celebrate the fact that he would probably differ with many aspects of our perspective on dialogue. (We have not been faithful followers.)

Kurt Lewin. Synchronicity worked for me again, as it had in distant Dar es Salaam when it led me to Paulo Freire, when I picked up Frank and David Johnson's book *Joining Together* (1987). The Johnson brothers have summarized the work of Kurt Lewin in a brilliant essay. I went back to Lewin's writings and recognized his importance in the development of a dialogue approach to teaching based on state-of-the-art principles.

In the basic JUBILEE course, learners do a set of learning tasks to master twelve principles for adult learning (described in full in Vella, 1996). What we call Lewin's Dozen is basic to quantum learning and disarmingly simple:

1. Effective learning will affect the learner's cognitive structures, attitudes and values and perceptions and behavioral patterns. That is, it always involves cognitive, affective and psychomotor factors.
2. People will believe more in knowledge they have discovered themselves than in knowledge presented by others.

3. Learning is more effective when it is an active rather than a passive process.

4. Acceptance of new ideas, attitudes and behavioral patterns cannot be brought about by a piecemeal approach—one's whole cognitive/affective/behavioral system (ideas/feelings/actions) has to change.

5. It takes more than information to change ideas, attitudes and behavioral patterns.

6. It takes more than firsthand experience to generate valid knowledge.

7. Behavior changes will be temporary unless the ideas and attitudes underlying them are changed.

8. Changes in perception of oneself and one's social environment are necessary before changes in ideas, attitudes and behavior will take place.

9. The more supportive, accepting and caring the social environment, the freer a person is to experiment with new behaviors, attitudes and ideas.

10. For changes in behavior patterns, attitudes and ideas to be permanent, both the person and the social environment have to change.

11. It is easier to change a person's ideas, attitudes and behavioral patterns when he or she accepts membership in a new group. The discussion and agreement that takes place within a group provides a personal commitment and encouragement for change that is not present when only one person is being changed.

12. A person accepts a new system of ideas, attitudes and behavioral patterns when he or she accepts membership in a new group. New groups with new role definitions and expectations for appropriate behavior are helpful in educational efforts [Johnson and Johnson, 1997, p. 54].

Lewin demonstrates in these principles what he learned as a soldier in World War II: the need for and potential of dialogue and the power of the small group.

Donald Oliver. Donald Oliver is, in my eyes, a peer of the both Lewin and Freire. His 1987 work *Education and Community* and his insightful *Education, Modernity and Fractured Meaning* (Oliver and Gershmann, 1987) provide a conceptual framework to understand why we teach through dialogue. His distinction between technical knowing and ontological knowing is operative whenever we use the dialogue approach. Serial thinking, as described above, leads to technical knowing. In our time, technical knowing is brilliant. The principles of dialogue education invite quantum thinking and ontological knowing. This kind of learning is what Freire meant by dialogue, as opposed to what he called "the banking system."

When we design appropriate and accountable learning tasks that engage adult learners in significant dialogue and ensure their learning the proposed content, we invite both technical and ontological knowing as Oliver defined it. He writes, "It is our thesis that healthy organisms, communities, societies must apprehend a universe/nature/culture that is balanced between these two qualities of knowing" (Oliver and Gershmann, 1987, p. 14).

Danah Zohar. In April 2000 a good friend sent me a copy of Zohar's *Rewiring the Corporate Brain* (1997). I did not touch it until a cold and rainy Memorial Day when I sat by the fire and read it with growing excitement from cover to cover. This was JUBILEE! We were inviting learners to do quantum learning and to celebrate quantum thinking, to see the world anew.

I recognized the JUBILEE dialogue approach throughout Zohar's management book. Inclusion, engagement, respect, doing and feeling and thinking, energy, dialogue, service, small groups, long-range planning for transformation, the use of the whole brain, music, art, and creativity—this approach for quantum learning is what I have been using and teaching since 1953 without knowing quite what it was. Zohar systemically compares and contrasts Newtonian science and the new science of quantum physics and invites leadership to contemplate the painful act of rewiring the corporate brain to use the new science. Such a rewired corporate brain will use the whole brain in planning and working, include everyone in an ongoing dialogue, consider the opportunities and potential of servant leadership in lieu of hierarchy, and live peacefully and confidently in the chaos of our current life.

I saw immediately how the JUBILEE approach to adult learning, using dialogue and not monologue, learning tasks and not teaching tasks, was parallel to the rewiring Zohar described and as painful a transformation. Tearing out the old wiring of assurance and certainty, right answers, closed questions, tests, and a teacher-centered approach hurts. When Zohar claimed that the tool for quantum thinking was dialogue, I knew we were working together. We had been inviting educators to grow new neural connectors (figuratively, of course) for years. Zohar's three ways of thinking—serial thinking, associative and parallel thinking, and quantum thinking—can all be evoked in well-designed learning tasks.

We use our energy (quanta) in serial thinking by making one-to-one connections, connecting neurons on a neural tract, as in the closed question, "What is the capital of New Jersey?" We use the energy (quanta) in patterned thinking by working the neural networks and seeing or organizing thought into patterns, as in this open question: "Look at this map of the United States. What do you notice about the location of state capitals?" And we can do quantum thinking by using a neural network of networks, the whole brain, creatively projecting, predicting, describing, envisioning, and inventing, as in this learning task: "Examine this map and description of our state capital and capital city. If you had the opportunity to redesign your state capital, what would you include in the city? Why?"

Implications for Adult Educators: Hard Work and Accountability

In the dialogue approach to teaching, we design so that that learning will take place during the session, whether that is a meeting, a seminar, a course, or a training session. In fact, the teaching is minimal: the new role of the "professor" is to prepare and set the learning task and to mentor the learners as they share their results. The new role of the professor in teaching as dialogue is as a resource person, a designer, an intense researcher, a listener, a clarifier, a celebrator, and a summarizer. He or she is engaged in learning-centered teaching and must work very hard at it.

What are the indicators of success in quantum learning effected by teaching through dialogue? You will see a unique level of excitement among learners, whose experience and creativity is being honored, perhaps for the first time. Learners will be questioning the theories and practices taught: How does this fit into my context? People will be bringing unique applications of the theories you teach, but also unique transformations of those theories and skills as they use them independently in their context. You will be accountable for your teaching.

We can grow to quantum learning. In a JUBILEE Advanced Design course recently, a community educator reluctantly admitted that he was using learning tasks in his designs, because that was what was expected in his agency. At the end of that course, this same educator said he would be using learning tasks in his designs for dialogue with the community because it was clear to him that this was an effective way to work. He had experienced quantum learning; he moved from serial thinking to quantum thinking through the three days of dialogue.

In terms of our accountability and the evaluation of our efforts at developing quantum learning through teaching through dialogue, we can be guided by this threefold matrix:

Learning takes place within the staff meeting, training session, course, seminar, or workshop by design. How do they know they know? They just did it, together and in a solo version.

Transfer takes place after the event, when the person is back at home or in the workplace or community. It is a repetition or paraphrasing of the knowledge, skills, or attitudes that were practiced in the learning session. We can invite people to celebrate transfer.

Impact is the change in the community, company, or person seen as a result of transfer and learning. It usually takes time to show impact. Name it, and celebrate it when you see it happening.

Here is an example of transfer. Not long after staff completed the Advanced Design course, the agency had a staff meeting to share data and opinions on their new offices. The director and her associates designed a dialogue learning task using the Seven Steps of Planning. The WHAT (content) was the design of the new offices, available in an architect's drawing. The WHO was the complete staff: ten men and women. The WHY (situation) was that they, the staff, needed an opportunity to respond to the initial plans from their unique and personal perspectives and to ask questions about the building process. The WHEN was forty-five minutes at lunch, and WHERE was the boardroom of the agency. The WHAT FOR covered the achievement-based objectives: "By the end of these forty-five minutes, all ten staff will have (1) heard a description of the building process of the new offices; (2) examined the draft architect's drawing in pairs; (3) identified and written their questions about the building process; (4) identified and shared their suggestions for changes in the plans; and (5) heard responses to some of the questions."

The director set out five learning tasks to go with each achievement-based objective, and the staff walked out after the lunch meeting quite excited and hopeful that they and their opinions had been heard. Questions that were not answered had been written so they could be responded to privately or in the next staff meeting. The whole session was carefully documented for future reference.

This event was a clear indicator of transfer of the learning that had taken place in the Advanced Design course. I propose the following indicators of impact: longer tenure of staff, joy in the workplace, creativity, open conflict and opposition, swift and thorough completion of project objectives, mentoring habits and the developing of mentoring relationships, new members brought in by present staff, and funds raised as a function of effective documentation.

What else would you want to see as impact on any of your work? It is your task to name that in the planning stage. The beginning and the end of educational design are connected.

Conclusion: Dialogue Moves Toward Quantum Learning

Dialogue is a quantum process, a means of doing and using quantum thinking (Zohar, 1997, p. 136).

Inviting dialogue by teaching through learning tasks assumes inclusion. We work in small groups so that everyone can be heard. Inclusion is an important principle for teaching as dialogue. I like the open question: Whom would you exclude? Those who are excluded from the ongoing dialogue in a company or a community are lost to that group. Their ideas might have been the most needed ones, and they are lost. Whom can we afford to exclude?

Imagine a society where teaching as dialogue is the norm. Consider the possibilities for inclusion in decision making, program design, and collaborative work. This applies to family, university, and corporate organizations. This is a move toward a more honest and comprehensive democracy.

The educational practices of a time are a clear and efficient mirror of the time. Quantum learning moves us toward a quantum society in which no one is excluded.

Autonomy is another linchpin of the dialogue approach to adult learning. In the either-or world of quantum thinking, the paradox of autonomous behavior at the service of the community is acceptable and understandable.

The dialogue approach to adult learning can be summarized in this way: learning tasks invite small, inclusive groups to a dialogue around the content being taught. This leads to accountable teaching and quantum learning within the teaching time frame. It celebrates the autonomy of the learner and the teacher alike.

On a planet struggling for its safety and life, where information is accessible to increasingly greater numbers of people, quantum learning is vital. As Zohar suggests, the means to quantum learning is dialogue. This is our challenge as teachers: Have we the humility and love to listen to the other half of the dialogue, to set learning tasks that stretch learners to the outskirts of themselves? Have we the courage to stop teaching and to concentrate on learning?

References

Bohm, D., and Peat, F. D. *Science, Order and Creativity*. New York: Bantam Books, 1987.
Campbell, J. *The Power of Myth*. New York: Doubleday, 1988.
Freire, P. *Pedagogy of the Oppressed*. New York: Continuum Publishing Company, 1993. (Originally published 1970.)
Johnson, D. W., and Johnson, F. P. *Joining Together*. (6th ed.) Upper Saddle River, N.J.: Prentice Hall, 1997.
Oliver, D., and Gershmann, K. W. *Education, Modernity and Fractured Meaning*. Albany, N.Y.: SUNY Press, 1987.
Vella, J. *Training Through Dialogue*. San Francisco: Jossey-Bass, 1996.
Zohar, D. *Rewiring the Corporate Brain*. San Francisco: Berrett-Koehler, 1997.

Additional Resources

Capra, F. F. *The Turning Point: Science, Society and Rising Culture*. New York: Bantam Books, 1983.
Hope, A., and Timmel, S. *Training for Transformation*. Washington, D.C.: Center for Concern, 1986.
Jaworski, J. *Synchronicity: The Inner Path of Leadership*. San Francisco: Berrett-Koehler, 1996.

Kindervatter, S. *Nonformal Education as an Empowering Process.* Amherst, Mass.: Center for International Education, 1979.

Kuhn, T. *Structure of a Scientific Revolution.* Chicago: University of Chicago Press, 1962.

Vella, J. *Learning to Listen, Learning to Teach.* San Francisco: Jossey-Bass, 1994.

Vella, J. *Taking Learning to Task.* San Francisco: Jossey-Bass, 2000.

Vella, J., Burrow J., and Berardinelli, P. *How Do They Know They Know?* San Francisco: Jossey-Bass 1997.

Wheatley, M. *Leadership and the New Science.* San Francisco: Berrett-Koehler, 1999.

JANE VELLA, the founder of JUBILEE Popular Education Center and Global Learning Partners, is an adjunct professor at the School of Public Health, University of North Carolina at Chapel Hill.

*This chapter integrates information from the previous
chapters to discuss several underlying themes and issues
related to effective teaching of adults.*

Effective Teaching of Adults: Themes and Conclusions

Jovita M. Ross-Gordon

As one of the core functions within adult and continuing-education practice, teaching continues to be a topic generating considerable discussion within the literature of the field (Apps, 1996; Brookfield, 1990, 1995; Draves, 1997; Palmer, 1998; Taylor, Marienau, and Fiddler, 2000). Each of the chapter authors in this volume has contributed to this conversation through one or more books published in the past decade (Cranton, 1994, 1998; Gadbow and Du Bois, 1998; Heimlich and Norland, 1994; Johnson-Bailey, 2001; Pratt and others, 1998; Vella, 1996, 2000; Zachary, 2000). Assembled together here, their ideas and suggestions encapsulate several of the key themes prominent in conceptions of teaching adults that have evolved since the publication of *Teaching Adults Effectively* (Knox, 1980) as one of the earliest volumes in this New Directions series.

Acknowledging the Validity of Multiple Perspectives on Teaching Adults

Moving beyond earlier debates over andragogy versus pedagogy, the chapters here reflect contemporary viewpoints that choices about teaching adults are and should be made based on numerous considerations, including factors related to content, learner background knowledge, and learner personal characteristics (Knowles, 1980; Grow, 1991, Pratt, 1988). To a greater extent than many previous discussions, Chapters One and Two in this volume

---

I thank Robert Rubeck and John Collins for their comments about and contributions to this chapter.

85

acknowledge the place of teacher beliefs and values as important influences on the selection of teaching approaches and strategies. In Chapter One, Pratt argues that while similar methods such as lecture or experiential learning may be employed by teachers holding differing perspectives, it is how they are used, and toward what ends, that most clearly differentiates among the five perspectives he and colleagues have identified. He advises readers to review the snapshots of each perspective, with a goal of locating their best fit with one or two perspectives. He maintains that each of these perspectives represents a legitimate view of teaching when enacted appropriately and promotes the idea that analysis of these perspectives can be used as in faculty development to help teachers identify, articulate, and justify their approach to teaching. Similarly, in Chapter Two, Heimlich and Norland review an extensive body of literature on teaching style. They stress that teaching style is not the same as teaching philosophy, but has more to do with achieving congruence between teaching practices and personal beliefs about elements of the teaching-learning exchange (teacher, learner, group, content, and environment). Like Apps in *Teaching from the Heart* (1996), Heimlich and Norland recommend that the analysis of our values about teaching and learning be placed in the context of a deeper analysis of who we are. Achieving congruence, as when a teacher realizes that despite her beliefs about the importance of active learning she spends the majority of class time using presentation methods, requires sometimes difficult decisions about changing beliefs, behaviors, both, or neither. The important message in both of these chapters is that there is no one right or wrong way of teaching adults. Teachers must continuously reflect on both their belief systems about teaching and learning and their teaching practices.

Reflecting on Beliefs and Practices

Reflective practice, a concept that many associate with the work of Donald Schön (1983), begins with the act of reflection. Both authors contributing to this volume and others not included here have stressed the importance of analyzing our beliefs and practices as a necessary first step toward becoming effective teachers of adults (Brookfield, 1995).

Reflecting on Adults as Learners. Each of Pratt's synopses of the five perspectives on teaching incorporates a metaphor for the adult learner (for example the container waiting to be filled with knowledge) as a way of clarifying the centrality of differing assumptions about adult learners to the diverse perspectives on teaching. Similarly, Heimlich and Norland include the learner as one of the five core elements comprising a model of the teaching-learning exchange. Although explicit discussion of adults as learners may be more apparent in some chapters than others, assumptions about adult learners undergird the approaches taken to the discussion of teaching by each of the contributing authors.

Reflecting on the Learning Process. Both Cranton (in Chapter Six) and Vella (in Chapter Seven) choose the discussion of adult learning as the starting point for their discussions of teaching. For Cranton, the increasingly prominent transformative learning theory serves as the foundation (Mezirow, 1991, 2000). Her explication of seven facets of the transformative learning process becomes the cornerstone for a discussion of teaching strategies aimed at assisting learners with each of these facets. For readers who long for examples, especially to concretize a concept-laden theory, Cranton's discussion should fit the bill. Vella draws on an interdisciplinary theoretical base to derive her own concept of quantum learning: "that which uses all of the neural networks in the brain, putting things together in idiosyncratic and personal ways to make significant meaning." To promote quantum thinking and learning, she advocates what she refers to as the dialogue approach to teaching, fashioned from the works of Dewey, Lewin, Knowles, and Freire, and crystallized out of her years of experience with diverse groups of adult learners and adult educators. Referring the reader to *Training Through Dialogue* (1996) for a complete discussion of the fifty principles and practices she has delineated as part of the dialogue approach, she presents here a core set of twelve principles referred to as "Lewin's Dozen."

Reflecting on the Teacher-Learner Relationship. Several of the authors have dealt directly or indirectly with the nature of teaching-learning relationships. In Chapter Three, Zachary explores the mentoring role and emphasizes the importance of relationship to successful enactment of that role. Extending the work of Daloz (1986, 1999) on the topic, Zachary delineates five evolutionary phases of the mentoring relationship (preparing oneself, preparing the relationship, negotiating, enabling, and coming to closure). Other chapters also deal with the teaching-learning relationship, even if in less obvious ways. Embedded in Pratt's discussion of five perspectives on teaching are assumptions about the relationship between teachers and adult learners, most explicit in the case of the nurturing perspective. Johnson-Bailey's discussion of race in Chapter Four as the invisible variable in the teaching-learning transaction challenges us to think in more conscious and more conscientious ways about the impact of positionality and privilege (or the relative lack thereof) on relationships between ourselves and our students, and even among our students. Gadbow's call in Chapter Five for responsive teaching suggests a more intimate teacher-student relationship that allows for getting to know the personal situations and needs of learners if we are to recognize and reduce the barriers they face.

Reflecting on the Social Context of Learning. In the past decade or so, increasing attention has been paid to the social and political context of adult learning and teaching, including systems of privilege that provide greater advantages to some adult learners than others (Johnson-Bailey and Cervero, 1998, 2000; Tisdell, 1993, 1995). In Chapter Four, Johnson-Bailey prompts us to consider how the social construct of race has been dealt with in both the literature on teaching adults and the environments of adult education classrooms or programs. After reviewing the color-blind and multicultural perspectives, which have dominated adult education literature and practice, Johnson-Bailey challenges us to shift to a social justice perspective that examines the ways that privilege and positionality affect the adult education curriculum, teaching practices, and classroom interactions. In describing how educators can begin this shift, she suggests that practitioners incorporate the following into their critical reflection on practice: "(1) a personal appraisal and understanding of their own cultural history, (2) a functional grasp of the sociopolitical forces that affect the learners and the learning environment, and (3) an evaluation of whether their own practice is part of the solution or part of the problem."

Gadbow's expansion of the concept of teaching for diversity to incorporate responding to learners' special needs and differences does not explicitly attend to concepts of power and privilege. Yet she encourages reflection on ways that various structural constraints built into programs limit opportunities for success, particularly for learners with visible and invisible disabilities. In addition to such accepted approaches as accommodations in learning methods and assessment and use of assistive technology, she calls for greater attention to the development of self-advocacy skills among learners who may have special learning needs.

Transforming Teaching Practices

Together, the chapters challenge us to follow up on reflection on our beliefs and practices by transforming our practice in ways consistent with our espoused beliefs. They also suggest ways to go about this transformation process in several core areas.

Promoting Reflection and Critical Thinking. A common thread in several chapters is the promotion of reflection and critical thinking among adult students, both through our own modeling of such practices and through our selection of teaching strategies designed to stimulate student growth and development. This is apparent in Chapter Six as Cranton discusses the role of critical reflection in the transformative learning process and makes explicit connections between selected teaching strategies (for example, critical incident, reflective journal, critical debates) and particular facets of the transformative learning process. Similarly, Lewin's Dozen, which Vella introduces, have direct applications to the promotion of critical reflection among learners as well as educators. Yet even in chapters that place less emphasis on the promotion of reflection and critical thinking among learners, connections are evident. For Johnson-Bailey, the work needed to transform the learning environment to reduce the effects of positionality and inequities in privilege will require that teachers and learners becomes partners in the effort to transform the learning environment. Similarly, both partners in the mentoring relationship that Zachary describes will need to engage in reflection and critical thinking if they are to navigate all five phases of the mentoring relationship successfully.

Teaching Responsively. The theme of teaching responsively is most obvious in Gadbow's chapter as she discusses the need to be responsive to individual learners' special learning needs. Yet the concept of responsiveness to learners' needs also is articulated in other chapters, sometimes using different language: the enabling phase of Zachary's mentoring relationships, Johnson-Bailey's call to make visible the invisible variable of race, and Pratt's review of the facilitation and nurturing perspectives. Indeed, the call to teach responsively is one of the threads that remains consistent with the era in adult education theory and practice when andragogy reigned supreme as the dominant theory of adult learning (Knowles, 1980).

Challenging the Status Quo. Among the five dominant perspectives on teaching that Pratt reviews is the social reform perspective, characterized by teachers who are working toward strong ideals and share a viewpoint that the ultimate goal of teaching is to bring about social change, not simply individual learning. In this perspective, classroom discussion is said to be "centered not on knowledge itself or how knowledge has been created, but by whom and for what purposes," and practices are interrogated "for what is said and what is not said, what is included and what is excluded, and who is represented and who is not represented in the dominant discourse of practice." Johnson-Bailey best exemplifies this perspective. Finding critical reflection to offer a promising direction to address issues of diversity and difference, she begins with reflection on her own positionality and her own classroom. She recommends an active role of the instructor in monitoring the power dynamics operating within the classroom and intervening to promote a democratic classroom environment. She challenges instructors to be part of the solution rather than part of the problem—through course content choices, inclusive classroom dialogues, and interrogation of the research of the field. Gadbow too advocates simultaneously addressing the barriers to successful learning embedded within our institutions, especially those affecting learners with disabilities, while teaching learners to negotiate the system through skilled self-advocacy.

Conclusion

Read as a totality, the chapters in this volume provide a succinct overview of many of the themes found in the current literature on teaching adults. They suggest that improving our effectiveness as teachers of adults begins with reflecting on our own beliefs about learners, the learning process, the teaching-learning relationship, and the social context in which the teaching-learning transaction occurs. While not providing a list of the technical do's and don'ts of effective adult instruction, they nonetheless provide practical guidance for aligning our teaching practices with our beliefs and for assisting learners to engage in similar reflection and critical thinking. I hope that this volume, used in conjunction with other excellent sources on specific techniques and strategies to use in teaching and training situations, will help committed professionals improve their effectiveness in the craft of teaching adults. In addition, those who seek to expand their knowledge will find it useful to continue their reading in this area, perhaps including the books published by the authors who have contributed to this volume, as well as drawing on the broader literature base reflected in the reference lists following each chapter.

References

Apps, J. W. *Teaching from the Heart*. Malabar, Fla.: Krieger, 1996.
Brookfield, S. D. *The Skillful Teacher*. San Francisco: Jossey-Bass, 1990.
Brookfield, S. D. *Becoming a Critically Reflective Teacher*. San Francisco: Jossey-Bass, 1995.
Cranton, P. *Understanding and Promoting Transformative Learning*. San Francisco: Jossey-Bass, 1994.
Cranton, P. *No One Way: Teaching and Learning in Higher Education*. Toronto: Wall & Emerson, 1998.
Daloz, L. *Effective Teaching and Mentoring*. San Francisco: Jossey-Bass, 1986.
Daloz, L. *Mentor: Guiding the Journey of Adult Learners*. San Francisco: Jossey-Bass, 1999.
Draves, W. A. *How To Teach Adults*. (2nd ed.) Manhattan, Kan.: Learning Resources Network, 1997.
Gadbow, N. F., and Du Bois, D. A. *Adult Learners with Special Needs: Strategies and Resources for Postsecondary Education and Workplace Training*. Malabar, Fla.: Krieger, 1998.
Grow, G. "Teaching Learners to Be Self-Directed: A Stage Approach." *Adult Education Quarterly*, 1991, *41*, 125–149.
Heimlich, J. E., and Norland, E. *Developing Teaching Style in Adult Education*. San Francisco: Jossey-Bass, 1994.
Johnson-Bailey, J. *Sistahs in College: Making a Way Out of No Way*. Malabar, Fla.: Krieger, 2001.
Johnson-Bailey, J., and Cervero, R. M. "Power Dynamics in Teaching and Learning Practices: An Examination of Two Adult Education Classrooms." *International Journal of Lifelong Education*, 1998, *17*, 389–399.
Johnson-Bailey, J., and Cervero, R. M. "The Invisible Politics of Race in Adult Education." In A. L. Wilson and E. R. Hayes (eds.), *Handbook of Adult and Continuing Education*. San Francisco: Jossey-Bass, 2000.
Knowles, M. S. *The Modern Practice of Adult Education: From Pedagogy to Andragogy*. (Rev. and updated.) River Grove, Ill.: Follett, 1980.
Knox, A. B. *Teaching Adults Effectively*. New Directions for Continuing Education, no. 6. San Francisco: Jossey-Bass, 1980.
Mezirow, J. *Transformative Dimensions of Adult Learning*. San Francisco: Jossey-Bass, 1991.
Mezirow, J., and others. *Learning as Transformation: Critical Perspectives on a Theory in Progress*. San Francisco: Jossey-Bass, 2000.
Palmer, P. J. *The Courage to Teach*. San Francisco: Jossey-Bass, 1998.
Pratt, D. D. "Andragogy as a Relational Construct." *Adult Education Quarterly*, 1988, *38*, 160–181.
Pratt, D. D., and others. *Five Perspectives on Teaching in Adult and Higher Education*. Malabar, Fla.: Krieger, 1998.
Schön, D. A. *The Reflective Practitioner: How Professionals Think in Action*. New York: Basic Books, 1983.
Taylor, K., Marienau, C., and Fiddler, M. *Developing Adult Learners: Strategies for Teachers and Trainers*. San Francisco: Jossey-Bass, 2000.

Tisdell, E. "Interlocking Systems of Power, Privilege, and Oppression in Adult Higher Education Classes." *Adult Education Quarterly,* 1993, *3,* 203–226.

Tisdell, E. *Creating Inclusive Adult Learning Environments: Insights from Multicultural and Feminist Pedagogy.* Columbus, Ohio: ERIC Clearinghouse on Adult, Career, and Vocational Education, 1995.

Vella, J. *Training Through Dialogue.* San Francisco: Jossey-Bass, 1996.

Vella, J. *Taking Learning to Task.* San Francisco: Jossey-Bass, 2000.

Zachary, L. *The Mentor's Guide: Facilitating Effective Learning Relationships.* San Francisco: Jossey-Bass, 2000.

JOVITA M. ROSS-GORDON is an associate professor in the College of Education at Southwest Texas State University, San Marcos.

INDEX

Americans with Disabilities Act of 1990, 55
Andragogy, 3, 28, 42, 57, 89
Apprenticeship view of teaching, 9–11
Apps, J., 40, 85, 86
Assumptions, underlying: articulating, 66, 67; revision of, 69–70
Autobiographies, student, 67
Axelrod, J., 18

Banks, J. A., 46
Beliefs and practices: changing, 20–23; reflecting on, 86–88
Bem, D. J., 22
Beziat, C., 53
Bohm, D., 76
Bohr, N., 76
Bosworth, K., 57
Brookfield, S. D., 18, 19, 28, 31, 40, 41, 45, 51, 57, 67, 68, 69, 85, 86
Brown, A., 43, 44
Brown, J. S., 9
Bruffee, K. A., 10
Budak, D., 22
Buddha, 75
Burch, M., 42

Cafferella, R. S., 42
Campbell, J., 75
Carter, T., 65
Cervero, R. M., 42, 44, 87
Chaiken, S., 21
Cohen, L., 67
Collard, S., 43
Collins, A., 9
Collins, J. B., 6
Color-blind perspective in adult education literature, 42
Communicative knowledge, 64
Constructivism, 5, 8
Conti, G. J., 17, 18
Cramer, S. F., 57
Cranton, P., 3, 63, 65, 85, 87, 88
Critical reflection: emancipatory knowledge from, 64; on race, 45–47, 88; in transformative learning, 3, 65, 66, 67–68; for transforming teaching practices, 88–89
Cross, K. P., 17

Cultural diversity perspective, 42–43
Cunningham, P. M., 39, 43

Daloz, L., 29, 34, 87
Davis, A. B., 1
Davis, J. R., 1
Deshler, D., 67
Developmental perspective on teaching, 8–9
Dewey, J., 74, 87
Dialogue approach to quantum learning: conclusions on, 81–82; description of, 74; evaluating efforts in, 80–81; and masters of quantum learning, 76–80; principles and practices of, 74–76
Dialogue journals, 69
Dirkx, J., 65
Disabilities, students with: statistics on, 53–54; technologies for, 58–59; traditional programs and, 54–56
Disability-related organizations, 59
Distance-learning programs, 52, 55, 56
Draves, W. A., 17, 20, 85
Du Bois, D., 52, 55, 56, 58, 85
Dunn, K. J., 17
Dunn, R. S., 17

Eagly, A. E., 21
Eble, K. E., 19
Edelman, M. W., 36
Emancipatory knowledge, 64
Emerson, R. W., 37
Enabling phase of mentoring process, 33–34, 35, 89

Fellenz, R. A., 1, 18
Fiddler, M., 1, 85
Fisher, B., 17
Fisher, L., 17
Flannery, D. D., 43
Fox, D., 5
Freire, P., 74, 76–77, 79, 87

Gadbow, N. F., 3, 52, 55, 56, 85, 87, 88, 89
Galbraith, M. W., 1, 30
Galvin, J. C., 58
Gauld, V. F., 17
Gershmann, K. W., 78, 79

Back Issue/Subscription Order Form

Copy or detach and send to:
Jossey-Bass, A Wiley Company, 989 Market Street, San Francisco CA 94103-1741

Call or fax tollfree: Phone 888-378-2537 6AM-5PM PST; Fax 800-605-2665

Back issues: Please send me the following issues at $27 each
(Important: please include series initials and issue number, such as ACE90)

1. ACE _____

_____

_____

$ _____Total for single issues

$ _____ SHIPPING CHARGES: SURFACE   Domestic   Canadian

	Domestic	Canadian
First Item	$5.00	$6.50
Each Add'l Item	$3.00	$3.00

For next-day and second-day delivery rates, call the number listed above.

Subscriptions: Please ❑ start ❑ renew my subscription to *New Directions for Adult and Continuing Education* for the year 2____ at the following rate:

U.S.	❑ Individual $65	❑ Institutional $135
Canada	❑ Individual $65	❑ Institutional $175
All Others	❑ Individual $89	❑ Institutional $209

$ _____Total single issues and subscriptions (Add appropriate sales tax for your state for single issue orders. No sales tax for U.S. subscriptions. Canadian residents, add GST for subscriptions and single issues.)
Federal Tax ID 135593032   GST 89102 8052

❑ Payment enclosed (U.S. check or money order only)

❑ VISA, MC, AmEx, Discover Card # _____ Exp. date_____

Signature _____ Day phone _____
❑ Bill me (U.S. institutional orders only. Purchase order required)
Purchase order #_____

Name _____
Address _____

_____

Phone_____ E-mail _____

For more information about Jossey-Bass, visit our Web site at: www.josseybass.com

PROMOTION CODE = ND3

ACE87 Team Teaching and Learning in Adult Education
Mary-Jane Eisen, Elizabeth J. Tisdell
The contributors show how team teaching can increase both organizational and individual learning in settings outside of a traditional classroom, for example, a recently deregulated public utility, a national literacy organization, and community-based settings such as Chicago's south side. They discuss how team teaching can be used in colleges and universities, describing strategies for administrators and teachers who want to integrate it into their curricula and classrooms.
ISBN 0-7879-5425-X

ACE86 Charting a Course for Continuing Professional Education: Reframing Professional Practice
Vivian W. Mott, Barbara J. Daley
This volume offers a resource to help practitioners examine and improve professional practice, and set new directions for the field of CPE across multiple professions. The contributors provide a brief review of the development of the field of CPE, analyze significant issues and trends that are shaping and changing the field, and propose a vision of the future of CPE.
ISBN 0-7879-5424-1

ACE85 Addressing the Spiritual Dimensions of Adult Learning: What Educators Can Do
Leona M. English, Marie A. Gillen
The contributors discuss how mentoring, self-directed learning, and dialogue can be used to promote spiritual development, and advocate the learning covenant as a way of formalizing the sanctity of the bond between learners and educators. Drawing on examples from continuing professional education, community development, and health education, they show how a spiritual dimension has been integrated into adult education programs.
ISBN 0-7879-5364-4

ACE84 An Update on Adult Development Theory: New Ways of Thinking About the Life Course
M. Carolyn Clark, Rosemary J. Caffarella
This volume presents discussions of well-established theories and new perspectives on learning in adulthood. Knowles' andragogy, self-directed learning, Mezirow's perspective transformation, and several other models are assessed for their contribution to our understanding of adult learning. In addition, recent theoretical orientations, including consciousness and learning, situated cognition, critical theory, and feminist pedagogy, are discussed in terms of how each expands the knowledge base of adult learning.
ISBN 0-7879-1171-2

ACE83 The Welfare-to-Work Challenge for Adult Literacy Educators
Larry G. Martin, James C. Fisher
Welfare reform and workforce development legislation has had a dramatic impact on the funding, implementation, and evaluation of adult basic education and literacy programs. This issue provides a framework for literacy practitioners to better align their field with the demands of the Work First environment and to meet the pragmatic expectations of an extended list of stakeholders.
ISBN 0-7879-1170-4

ACE82 Providing Culturally Relevant Adult Education: A Challenge for the
Twenty-First Century
Talmadge C. Guy
This issue offers more inclusive theories that focus on how learners
construct meaning in a social and cultural context. Chapters identify ways
that adult educators can work more effectively with racially, ethnically, and
linguistically marginalized learners, and explore how adult education can be
an effective tool for empowering learners to take control of their
circumstances.
ISBN 0-7879-1167-4

ACE81 Enhancing Creativity in Adult and Continuing Education: Innovative
Approaches, Methods, and Ideas
Paul Jay Edelson, Patricia L. Malone
The authors discuss innovations in a variety of continuing education
settings, including the Harvard Institute for the Management of Lifelong
Education; a drug and alcohol prevention program; and a college degree
program developed through the collaboration of the Bell Atlantic
Corporation and a consortium of community colleges.
ISBN 0-7879-1169-0

ACE79 The Power and Potential of Collaborative Learning Partnerships
Iris M. Saltiel, Angela Sgroi, Ralph G. Brockett
This volume draws on examples of collaborative partnerships to explore the
many ways collaboration can generate learning and knowledge. The
contributors identify the factors that make for strong collaborative
relationships, and they reveal how these partnerships actually help learners
generate knowledge and insights well beyond what each brings to the
learning situation.
ISBN 0-7879-9815-X

ACE78 Adult Learning and the Internet
Brad Cahoon
This volume explores the effects of the Internet on adult learning—both as
that learning is facilitated through formal instruction and as it occurs
spontaneously in the experiences of individuals and groups—and provides
guidance to adult and continuing educators searching for ways to use the
Internet effectively in their practice.
ISBN 0-7879-1166-6

ACE77 Using Learning to Meet the Challenges of Older Adulthood
James C. Fisher, Mary Alice Wolf
Combining theory and research in educational gerontology with the practice
of older adult learning and education, this volume explores issues related to
older adult education in academic and community settings. It is designed for
educators and others concerned with the phenomenon of aging in America
and with the continuing development of the field of educational
gerontology.
ISBN 0-7879-1164-X

ACE76 New Perspectives on Designing and Implementing Effective Workshops
Jean Anderson Fleming
Provides workshop leaders with the information necessary to hone their
skills in everything from planning and instructional design to delivery and

evaluation. Seasoned workshop veterans give practical suggestions to help
professionals navigate the challenges and exploit the potential of distance
learning; effectively use technology and the media; and negotiate power
dynamics in the intensity of the workshop atmosphere.
ISBN 0-7879-1163-1

ACE75   **Assessing Adult LearnFing in Diverse Settings: Current Issues and
        Approaches**
        Amy D. Rose, Meredyth A. Leahy
        Examines assessment approaches analytically from different programmatic
        levels and looks at the implications of these differing approaches. Chapters
        discuss the implications of cultural differences as well as ideas about
        knowledge and knowing and the implications these ideas can have for both
        the participant and the program.
        ISBN 0-7879-9840-0

ACE73   **Creating Practical Knowledge Through Action Research: Posing Problems,
        Solving Problems, and Improving Daily Practice**
        B. Allan Quigley, Gary W. Kuhne
        Outlines the process of action research step-by-step, provide a convenient
        project planner, and presents examples to show how action research yielded
        improvements in six different settings, including a hospital, a university and
        a literacy education program.
        ISBN 0-7879-9841-9

ACE70   **A Community-Based Approach to Literacy Programs: Taking Learners'
        Lives into Account**
        Peggy A. Sissel
        Encouraging a community-based approach that takes account of the reality
        of learner's lives; this volume offers suggestions for incorporating knowledge
        about a learner's particular context, culture, and community into adult
        literacy programming.
        ISBN 0-7879-9867-2

ACE69   **What Really Matters in Adult Education Program Planning: Lessons in
        Negotiating Power and Interests**
        Ronald M. Cervero, Arthur L. Wilson
        Identifies issues faced by program planners in practice settings and the
        actual negotiation strategies they use. Argues that planning is generally
        conducted within a set of personal, organizational, and social relationships
        among people who may have similar, different, or conflicting interests and
        the program planner's responsibility centers on how to negotiate these
        interests to construct an effective program.
        ISBN 0-7879-9866-4

ACE68   **Workplace Learning**
        W. Franklin Spikes
        Increased technology, new management strategies, and reengineered and
        downsized organizations have caused workplace educators to rethink their
        craft and formulate answers to the new and immediate business issues faced
        by their organizations. This volume is designed to help readers examine
        current issues surrounding workplace learning programs and incorporate
        these ideas into their own professional practice.
        ISBN 0-7879-9937-7

OTHER TITLES AVAILABLE IN THE
NEW DIRECTIONS FOR COMMUNITY COLLEGES SERIES
Arthur M. Cohen, Editor-in-Chief
Florence B. Brawer, Associate Editor

CC115 The New Vocationalism in Community Colleges, *Debra D. Bragg*

CC114 Transfer Students: Trends and Issues, *Frankie Santos Laanan*

CC113 Systems for Offering Concurrent Enrollment at High Schools and Community Colleges, *Piedad F. Robertson, Brian G. Chapman, Fred Gaskin*

CC112 Beyond Access: Methods and Models for Increasing Retention and Learning Among Minority Students, *Steven R. Aragon*

CC111 How Community Colleges Can Create Productive Collaborations with Local Schools, *James C. Palmer*

CC110 Building Successful Relationships Between Community Colleges and the Media, *Clifton Truman Daniel, Hanel Henriksen Hastings*

CC109 Dimensions of Managing Academic Affairs in the Community College, *Douglas Robillard, Jr.*

CC108 Trends in Community College Curriculum, *Gwyer Schuyler*

CC107 Gateways to Democracy: Six Urban Community College Systems, *Raymond C. Bowen, Gilbert H. Muller*

CC106 Understanding the Impact of Reverse Transfer Students on Community Colleges, *Barbara K. Townsend*

CC105 Preparing Department Chairs for Their Leadership Roles, *Rosemary Gillett-Karam*

CC104 Determining the Economic Benefits of Attending Community College, *Jorge R. Sanchez, Frankie Santos Laanan*

CC103 Creating and Benefiting from Institutional Collaboration: Models for Success, *Dennis McGrath*

CC102 Organizational Change in the Community College: A Ripple or a Sea Change? *John Stewart Levin*

CC101 Integrating Technology on Campus: Human Sensibilities and Technical Possibilities, *Kamala Anandam*

CC100 Implementing Effective Policies for Remedial and Developmental Education, *Jan M. Ignash*

CC99 Building a Working Policy for Distance Education, *Connie L. Dillon, Rosa Cintron*

CC98 Presidents and Trustees in Partnership: New Roles and Leadership Challenges, *Iris M. Weisman, George B. Vaughan*

CC97 School-to-Work Systems: The Role of Community Colleges in Preparing Students and Facilitating Transitions, *Edgar I. Farmer, Cassy B. Key*

CC96 Transfer and Articulation: Improving Policies to Meet New Needs, *Tronie Rifkin*

CC95 Graduate and Continuing Education for Community College Leaders: What It Means Today, *James C. Palmer, Stephen G. Katsinas*

CC93 Promoting Community Renewal Through Civic Literacy and Service Learning, *Michael H. Parsons, C. David Lisman*

CC89 Gender and Power in the Community College, *Barbara K. Townsend*

CC77 Critical Thinking: Educational Imperative, *Cynthia A. Barnes*

OTHER TITLES AVAILABLE IN THE
NEW DIRECTIONS FOR TEACHING AND LEARNING SERIES
Marilla D. Svinicki, Editor-in-Chief
R. Eugene Rice, Consulting Editor